'Contemporary liberal thought imagines war as a perpetual policing exercise, in which disorder is made into order. Demonstrating a command of theory few analysts of war can muster, Holmqvist shows how liberalism supplies a set of metaphors – an intellectual scaffolding encompassing time, space, agency and power – through which war becomes a management tool for the restoration of the social contract in other peoples' countries. While real in its effects, such imagination amounts to an illusory construct of war, with results for all to see in Iraq and Afghanistan. Surpassing earlier analyses of liberal war in depth and sophistication, Holmqvist is now the definitive guide.'

— **Tarak Barkawi**, *London School of Economics and Political Science, UK*

'War without antagonism is one of the great oxymorons for our time. Holmqvist explores the sense in western military theory that war can be fought without ultimate opposition when it is about reducing disorder and policing good governance. Those who resist this oxymoronic post-adversarial logic get branded and punished as obstructionist criminal elements. Holmqvist stretches the concept of contemporary war as a form of policing liberal order by tracing its roots to pre-9/11 times and spaces and by theorising its depths today. She is a compelling and important new voice on the forms, logics and implications of today's western ways of warring.'

— **Christine Sylvester**, *University of Connecticut, USA*

This interdisciplinary study provides an original account of the US-led wars in Afghanistan and Iraq to show how, why and with what consequences, twenty-first century wars became seen as policing wars. Holmqvist starts from the assumption that wars always reflect the societies that wage them and combines the analysis of Western strategic thinking with a philosophical examination of the core ideas that structure the contemporary liberal imagination. She argues that the US-led interventions in Afghanistan and Iraq were characterised by a widespread understanding of war as 'policing' – that is, waged against opponents deemed 'criminal' rather than political, and directed at the creation and maintenance of a certain type of 'order'. Holmqvist turns to themes of social theory and philosophy to offer new perspectives on why the wars in Afghanistan and Iraq were waged in the way they were, and why the fantasy of policing wars came to resonate so widely amongst policy makers and academics alike. This unique contribution to the study of war and international politics will appeal to scholars of the philosophy and sociology of war, military strategy and international relations.

**Caroline Holmqvist** is Senior Lecturer in War Studies at the Swedish National Defence College in Stockholm, Sweden and a Visiting Fellow at the Centre for International Studies at the London School of Economics, UK. She has previously worked at the Stockholm Institute for International Affairs and at the Stockholm International Peace Research Institute.

*Rethinking Political Violence Series*

Series editor: **Roger Mac Ginty**, Professor of Peace and Conflict Studies, University of Manchester, UK

This exciting series provides a space in which to interrogate and challenge much of the conventional wisdom on political violence. Books in the series are at the forefront of research, pushing forward new debate in the field of political violence without rehashing clichés about security, violence and 'terrorism'. Authors from both the critical and orthodox perspectives use the book series to reappraise some of the fundamental questions facing societies on how to deal with and interpret organised violence. Many of the books in the series are comparative, draw on fieldwork, and use insights from a variety of methodologies.

*Titles include*:

Stephen Gibson and Simon Mollan (*editors*)
REPRESENTATIONS OF PEACE AND CONFLICT

Linda A. Hall and Laura J. Shepherd (*editors*)
GENDER, AGENCY AND POLITICAL VIOLENCE

Caroline Holmqvist
POLICING WARS
On Military Intervention in the Twenty-First Century

Jaremey R. McMullin
EX-COMBATANTS AND THE POST-CONFLICT STATE
Challenges of Reintegration

Rethinking Political Violence series
Series Standing Order ISBN 978–0–230–24376–7

You can receive future titles in this series as they are published by placing a standing order. Please contact your bookseller or, in case of difficulty, write to us at the address below with your name and address, the title of the series and the ISBN quoted above.

Customer Services Department, Macmillan Distribution Ltd, Houndmills, Basingstoke, Hampshire RG21 6XS, England

# Policing Wars

## On Military Intervention in the Twenty-First Century

Caroline Holmqvist
*Swedish National Defence College, Stockholm, Sweden*

**palgrave**
macmillan

ISBN 978-1-349-99990-3     ISBN 978-1-137-32362-0 (eBook)
DOI 10.1007/978-1-137-32362-0

First published 2014 by
PALGRAVE MACMILLAN

Palgrave Macmillan in the UK is an imprint of Macmillan Publishers Limited, registered in England, company number 785998, of Houndmills, Basingstoke, Hampshire RG21 6XS.

Palgrave Macmillan in the US is a division of St Martin's Press LLC, 175 Fifth Avenue, New York, NY 10010.

Palgrave Macmillan is the global academic imprint of the above companies and has companies and representatives throughout the world.

Palgrave® and Macmillan® are registered trademarks in the United States, the United Kingdom, Europe and other countries.

ISBN 978-1-137-32360-6

This book is printed on paper suitable for recycling and made from fully managed and sustained forest sources. Logging, pulping and manufacturing processes are expected to conform to the environmental regulations of the country of origin.

A catalogue record for this book is available from the British Library.

A catalog record for this book is available from the Library of Congress.

Typeset by MPS Limited, Chennai, India.

# Contents

# Preface and Acknowledgements

This is not a book about policing. Nor is it, really, a book about war. Instead, it is an attempt to describe how a certain rationalisation of war – of war *as* policing, directed against purportedly 'criminal' forces and in the interest of upholding a particular type of 'order' – came to resonate so widely in the first decade of the twenty-first century. More than anything, it is an attempt to approach the study of war by looking at what sustains particular ideas, rationalisations and imaginations of war, and asking why certain ideas (about war) catch on when they do.

The US-led wars in Afghanistan and Iraq came to stand at the pivot of debates about war from the time of the original invasions in 2001 and 2003 respectively. For sure, they were a part of the 'war on terror', but they also had many other origins – and they fit in with particular ideas about the world, politics and change. This book turns to themes of social theory and philosophy to offer new perspectives on why these wars were conducted in the way they were, and why so many people at the time seemed to partake in the fantasy of war as 'policing'.

This book is originally my PhD thesis, and the greatest thanks I owe are to Professor Christopher Coker and Professor Mervyn Frost, my two supervisors. Both were extremely generous, helpful and above all inspiring. Encouragement from my friends Dan Öberg, Tom Lundborg, Astrid Nordin and Stefan Borg of the Stockholm International Theory Group was important during the time I took to rewrite the thesis into a book.

Parts of Chapter 2 were published previously in *The Character of War in the 21st Century*, Eds Caroline Holmqvist and Christopher Coker (London: Routledge, 2010), and parts of Chapter 3 appeared in an article in the journal *Global Crime*, vol. 13 no. 4 (2012). I am grateful to Taylor & Francis for allowing me permission to reprint this material.

My sincere thanks go to Roger Mac Ginty, editor of *Rethinking Political Violence*, for inviting me to contribute this book to the series; to Julia Willan, Eleanor Davey-Corrigan and Harriet Barker at

Palgrave for their help along the way with all aspects of the project; and to Geetha Williams for excellent project management. My friend Jens Münch shot the cover image in Iraq in 2003; I'm very glad he allowed me to use it for this book. The photograph was taken on 17 February 2003 on the northbound motorway from Kuwait City, leading up to border with Iraq.

Finally, I'd like to thank my husband, Staffan, who has witnessed this project from PhD to book – via a stint in Kabul, Afghanistan in 2009 and two periods of leave from work with the arrival of our children Clara and Sofus in 2010 and 2013. I'm grateful for a great many things in our life together but right now most of all for his urging me to 'get the book done'.

# Introduction

In 2009 General David Petraeus was voted 'public intellectual of the year' by the British liberal arts magazine *Prospect*, triumphing over names like Noam Chomsky, Francis Fukuyama and Slavoj Žižek. The magazine's motivation was that the United States Counterinsurgency Field Manual COIN FM 3–24, of which Petraeus was the lead author, was seen to constitute 'the first actively humane war fighting doctrine ever to come out of the Pentagon, enshrining the ideas that winning a modern war requires ensuring the security and wellbeing of the civilian population'.[1] The COIN way of warfare, it appears, is in tune with the Zeitgeist; the Field Manual has reportedly been downloaded over two million times a year after its release in 2006.[2] With its emphasis on social, economic and political 'governance' it constitutes the most recent reincarnation of liberal interventionism. And for the purposes of this study, it epitomises the narration of war as an order-creating force, as 'policing', metaphorically understood.

This is a study of how liberal states rationalised war in the first decade of the twenty-first century. As such, it is necessarily as much a study of the contemporary liberal world itself as it is a study of war alone. As the renowned historian of war Azar Gat tells us, understanding war is an indispensable part of understanding the constitution and evolution of societies: 'with war being connected to everything else and everything else being connected to war, explaining war and tracing its development in relation to human development in general almost amounts to a theory and history of everything'.[3] War constitutes a fundamentally social activity; intimately connected with social upheaval and change, it touches the deepest of human

1

emotions through life–death encounter. Studying the rationalisation of war thus helps us to understand the societies that wage war – the ideas and ideals professed by political and military leaders and the conceptual categories on which they rely for the understanding of social life, of politics and of war.

Two wars more than any others shaped liberal debates on war and strategic thinking in the first decade of the twenty-first century: those in Afghanistan and Iraq. Under the aegis of the United States and the United Kingdom, the interventions have been substantial undertakings: multinational forces in Iraq peaked at 183,000 troops in 2005, while the number deployed as part of the International Security Assistance Force (ISAF) in Afghanistan stood at 130,000 in 2011.[4] In human and material terms, the campaigns in Afghanistan and Iraq have been massive. The toll on civilian populations in both countries has been devastating. In moral and ideational terms, the military campaigns remain at the centre of debates about the form and character of global security politics in a decade that opened with the 9/11 attacks and the positing of 'terrorism' as the defining feature of a purportedly new security climate. The wars in Afghanistan and Iraq have been pivotal in shaping discussions about the global political realm and the driving forces of global change. In short, these wars epitomised a particular rationalisation of war that emerged in the opening decade of a new century. This specific rationalisation – with which this book is centrally concerned – follows a logic which I call that of *policing wars.*

*Policing war* is used to express the way in which military intervention has been thought and enacted as a means of fundamentally *re-ordering societies* through the conjoining of large-scale military intervention with an equally large or larger civilian presence dedicated to establishing democratic institutions and promoting 'good governance' according to Western standards. This broad shift has taken various expressions throughout the years: from the merging of security and development policies since the beginning of the 1990s and the development of a plethora of structures and policies under the umbrella of 'liberal interventionism', to the resurgence in interest in counterinsurgency as military strategy and doctrine.[5] The interventions in Iraq and Afghanistan led by the US and the UK emerged as paradigmatic for twenty-first-century warfare: their significance and standing in the global political/security agenda came to far exceed the scope of the interventions 'themselves'. They came to represent, in short, the way in which military activity on the part of liberal states in Afghanistan and Iraq was now being rationalised as essentially concerned with the creation of a specific type of social and political order in the societies in which they intervened – and, most importantly, the conviction that such endeavours were motivated and plausible; and that their cause and conduct was, as *Prospect* readers were told, 'actively humane'. At the heart of this narrative is the notion that 'war' nowadays take place not for lofty power political purposes but is conceived as a *corrective* directed against *enemies of order* – those who contest the new social and political order. Who, the logic goes, could be opposed to the promotion of democracy or the establishment of 'good governance', especially when set against the dystopia of 'terrorism', 'state failure', 'disorder' and 'insurgency'? This is the irresistible illusion of the *policing wars* narrative: the illusion that warfighting not only is compatible with the advancement of such goals, but that it indeed promotes it.[6]

Liberal intervention/ism (and liberal internationalism) has of course been the subject of much critical academic debate.[7] While this debate has been far-ranging, productive and stimulating, it has suffered from a general endeavour to critically assess all aspects of liberal interventionism simultaneously, from the humanitarian to the military. In contrast, this book focuses on the *war logic* of liberal interventions/interventionism: *the thinking and rationale underpinning the use of military force*. This book seeks to unravel the way in which thinking about *war itself* has changed as a result of the ideological quests of liberal interventionism and liberal internationalism. This includes posing questions such as: what understanding of war is promoted by the fusion of war-fighting with the advancement of a liberal humanitarian, state-building, security-and-development promoting agenda? What view of military force and the lethal confrontation that is *war* is enabled or generated by its being subsumed under the liberal interventionist umbrella? How, in short, is *the phenomenon of war* thought of in the context of twenty-first century liberal interventionism?

Conspicuously absent from this discussion, of course, is the term 'war' itself. Wars are no longer 'declared' (neither the UK nor the US have declared war since their entry into the Second World War in 1939 and 1941 respectively). In political discourse, the term 'war' is rarely used – instead, reference is made to 'peace operations', 'stabilisation', or 'counterinsurgency'; in short, to a whole plethora of terms that euphemise the activity of war. This euphemisation is not simply hypocritical (as for instance Noam Chomsky might argue): it is indicative of a wider shift in the logics resorted to in order to rationalise war-fighting itself. War has not *become* liberal interventionism: rather, war and war-fighting have become interpreted through the lens of liberal internationalist ideals. The result, I argue in this book, is that war itself has become understood metaphorically *as policing*. From Tony Blair's ambition to 'build an Afghanistan as strong as the coalition to defeat the Taliban' or George W. Bush's proclamation of an agenda 'freedom and independence, security and prosperity for the Iraqi people', to Barack Obama's desire to 'advance security, opportunity, and justice in Afghanistan', liberal leaders have sought to infuse war-fighting with humanitarian, democracy-promoting, state-building aims, to a point where these aims are put forth unproblematically as *intrinsic to war*.[8] In this context, concepts conventionally associated with war lose meaning and 'war' ceases to be a discrete event. The wars of the twenty-first century have thus become *policing wars*.

Though this is primarily a policy discourse set in motion by, but by no means limited to, the George W. Bush and Tony Blair administrations, there are notable expressions of the policing war reasoning in mainstream academic discourse. In his 2008 article 'Are we at war?' celebrated military historian Michael Howard described the realm of the global as one of 'disorder', arguing that 'our [liberal states] approach in dealing with them should not be that of "warriors" but of police, whose function is the preservation of civil order and for whom the use of force is the last and least desirable resort'.[9] In John Mueller's rendition, twenty-first-century war is 'reduced to its pathetic, if often highly destructive remnants' where only 'criminal warfare' remains. Mueller sees this as ushering in a 'new era of remarkable consensus' where 'developed countries apply military force – that is, war – to police [these remnants of war]'.[10] The policing war narrative as it emerged both in policy discourse and mainstream conflict research (discussed in detail in Chapter 1) can thus be summarised as follows: first, the notion that war in the first decade of the twenty-first century is waged by the liberal world as a necessary corrective to the unlawful behaviour of 'criminal', 'terrorist' others;

second, that it is, in fact, possible to effect social change in a target society in the context of war; and third, the notion that war can indeed be a useful instrument in the creation of social order – in other words, that there is no essential contradiction between 'war' and 'policing'.

## Distinctions, distinctions: war and policing

There is no universally accepted definition of war. Notwithstanding the strides taken in establishing universal laws of war, whether or not a situation qualifies as 'war' is often a source of contention. For instance, for a party to a conflict to be recognised as a warring party under international humanitarian law, its members need to wear uniform and be subject to a unified command – criteria that are unmet in many conflicts from Colombia to Somalia, the North Caucasus or Pakistan. Statisticians of war insist that war can be defined and that consequently its incidence and duration can be measured by objective standards, but their attempts at constructing scientific definitions of war remain contentious. In one oft-cited example, a 'warring party' needs to have a 'stated incompatibility' with a government over either the control of government or the control of territory in order for the situation in question to qualify as 'conflict' at all – a definition that excludes situations where aims may bypass the geographical state altogether (a topic which will be discussed in detail in Chapter 3).[11] Likewise, periodic attempts to provide definitive conceptualisations of war are notoriously short-lived: attempts such as Mary Kaldor's distinction between 'new' and 'old' wars, labels of 'asymmetric war', '4th generation warfare', 'complex irregular warfare', 'hybrid war' and so on all rapidly waxed and waned.[12]

Describing war simply as the activity carried out by state military forces is clearly an oversimplification, yet the institutional embodiment of the use of force has played an important role in shaping modern conceptions of war and continues to shape expectations today. The conventional modern understanding distinguishes between force used for the state's protection against external aggression – the remit of state military forces – and the use of force designated to maintain domestic order – the responsibility of a national police. Capturing both functions, Max Weber memorably located the essential identity of the modern state in its possession of a 'monopoly on the legitimate use of force'.[13] In this rendition, the military and the police are naturally distinct, both as regards the tasks or activities each can legitimately undertake and the overall purpose or function of respective institution. Anthony Giddens similarly posits the distinction of *raison d'être* between military and police as crucial to the emergence of the modern nation-state itself – 'a symbol and material expression of this phenomenon'.[14] Internal pacification and the subsequent consolidation of internal administrative resources followed closely in the modern (European) state's development. Conceptually then, the military–police distinction is an external–internal one, demarcated by the borders of the sovereign state – a distinction relevant not only in themselves, but equally for the international system of states which still formally rests on principles of sovereignty and non-interference.[15]

Concerned with the maintenance of domestic law and order, police are thus thought to direct their presence and action not simply against those who transgress the law – delinquents or criminals – but against society as a whole, in the sense that they uphold order in general. This maintenance of civil order is carried out under an agreed authority, the state, and police are equally interested in preventing, detecting and investigating crime. Police and military as ideal types thus operate under fundamentally different logics: the police implement a known body of law under which certain actions are criminal. This is manifest in the licence to deprive a person of their liberty and place them under arrest. Military power, on the other hand, is, in Hans Morgenthau's words, the *ultima ratio* of state power: the action of militaries is conventionally directed against external enemy forces as opposed to being directed against individuals.[16] The clash of force that constitutes war does not take place under clear authority in any way comparable to policing of domestic civil society – the regimes of the laws of war and the existence of the United Nations notwithstanding. Police, in most states, face important constraints on the use of deadly force. Military forces, conversely, do have an understood right to kill (though this is of course limited by *in bello* laws). The 'non-restriction' of the use of force (allowing for a right to kill) is thus a central feature of war – central also to the way in which the phenomenon has historically been understood.

It has become fashionable to claim that the modern distinction between 'military' and 'police' or, indeed, between 'war' and 'policing', is becoming blurred. New empirical realities have spawned such claims: for instance, the international deployment of national police, both as part of United Nations-mandated operations and as ad hoc missions, has been termed a 'new international policing'.[17] The transitional administrations of Kosovo and East Timor under United Nations' mandates constitute *par excellence* examples: responsibility of enforcing the law was left to UNMIK (United Nations Interim Administration Mission in Kosovo) and UNTAET (United Nations Transitional Administration in East Timor) respectively. In some contexts, of course, the modern military–police distinction was never instituted in practice, as military rule in many Latin American states testify.[18] Moreover, practices of 'international policing' can be located in the context of a wider internationalisation of crime control, as increased international cooperation between law enforcement agencies has left external police agencies to penetrate deep into (other) sovereign states in pursuit of drug traffickers or transnational terrorist networks.[19] Such developments notwithstanding (while it is physically possible to deploy national police forces internationally), the act of policing does not hold literal meaning on the global level, for the simple reason that there is no overarching authority whose law would be enforced through police action. There is, in Hobbes' terms, no Leviathan. Every use of the notion of 'policing' to extend beyond the sovereign state thus rests on a certain measure of figural speech.

This is true, of course, of the reference to the trope of 'empire' and the accompanying notion of 'policing'. In its exercise of physical, material and territorial power, the imperial state subjugated conquered states to imperial rule in a literal rather than metaphorical sense. Such *de facto* imperial policing has inspired use of the trope of 'empire' in critical debates on war in recent years – most prominently perhaps in Michael Hardt and Antonio Negri's *Empire* (2000).[20] Several factors distinguish the notion of *policing war* as here set out from Hardt and Negri's notion of 'empire', and the sources of the logic of war are sought in very different ways from that presented in *Empire*. Whereas Hardt and Negri explain an underlying biopolitical logic, this book is concerned with the ways in which a particular understanding, narrative and rationalisation of war emerged among policymakers and in mainstream academia and conflict research in the decades since the end of the Cold War, and was put into

practice in the interventions in Afghanistan and Iraq. Central to the policing wars narrative is a particular understanding of political confrontation – a theme which runs through the book as a whole but will be briefly introduced in the section to follow.

## Policing logics: war 'without antagonism'

A key trait of the *policing war* logic is its assumption of feasibility: it is assumed that a specific type of order *can* in fact be created through military intervention by external forces. Conversely, there is assumed to be no contradiction between war-fighting and 'democracy-promotion', 'state-building', 'capacity-building', and so on. Instead such concepts have become the very foundation of strategic and doctrinal guidance in recent years, culminating in the overwhelming reception of Petreaus' counterinsurgency doctrine in 2006. Crucially, the policing war discourse breaks with classic understandings of war, which emphasise the notion of confrontation, clash and conflict. Carl von Clausewitz' pivotal statement on war, made on the first page of *On War*, establishes war as 'an act of force that compels the enemy to do our will'.[21] Clausewitz' phenomenology showed antagonism to be essential, intrinsic, to war; whatever else war *is*, it is antagonistic, confrontational, coercive. Clausewitz' phenomenology builds in turn on Hegel's and in recent efforts to resurrect the phenomenological study of war, Tarak Barkawi and Shane Brighton seize on this lineage as they suggest that 'fighting' should be seen to have 'ontological primacy' for understanding war. The 'fighting' they refer to is *more than* mere kinetic exchange or its imminent possibility: in Barkawi and Brighton's reading, fighting's *excess* is what makes war irreducible to the instrumentalist readings offered by classic strategists, and the phenomenon of war both constitutive and generative.[22]

What I call policing wars, on the contrary, are wars imagined to be free from antagonism. Because the goals they set up (of 'democracy', 'good governance' and so on) are not simply goals but *endemic to the very imagination of war itself*, the logic enshrined in policing wars is that of a war without political opposition – *a war without conflict*. This fantasy is what compels statements like the one of then UK Prime Minister Gordon Brown about the war in Afghanistan in 2009: 'There can be only one winner,' Brown admonished, 'democracy and a strong Afghan state.'[23] Brown's statement epitomises the illusion of war without 'real' opposition or antagonism: to the liberal objectives of 'democracy' and 'good governance' *there can be no real opposition.* The manifestation and sources of such imagination are explored throughout this book, with different facets and features uncovered in Chapters 2, 3, 4 and 5 respectively. In Chapters 4 and 5 we shall see how they link up with what has been called the post-political age at large, trumpeted by writers such as Anthony Giddens, Ulrich Beck and Zygmunt Bauman, and roundly critiqued by Chantal Mouffe and others. Exploring the absence of politics or the imagination of *apolitical war* in the policing wars narrative is central to the discussion of the way in which the logic of policing war came into existence in the first place, and how it came to resonate so widely among policymakers and mainstream academics in the first decade of the twenty-first century. In order to uncover the origins and manifestation of this narrative, we need to situate military thinking in a wider context than commonly done. As Azar Gat reminds us, the ways in which societies conceive of and wage war tell us something fundamental about those societies, about the culture that prevails and about the ways in which collective imaginations take hold. In order to make sense of the policing wars logic, this book suggests we should think of the conflation of 'war' and 'policing' as being of a metaphorical kind: thinking one concept *in terms of* another.

## Metaphorical thinking

Betrand Russell once wrote of the study of grammar that he found it to be capable of throwing far more light on philosophical questions than what is commonly supposed by philosophers.[24] Examination of the metaphors that colour discourse, in other words, is meritorious: it tells us something about the way in which human beings seek to invest the world around them with meaning. This is a classic preoccupation of the hermeneutic tradition of social thought, uniting inquiries around a shared concern for ontological questions of Being and asking questions along the lines of 'why is the world is the way it is; why do we believe the things we do, in the way we do?'[25] In contrast to the instrumental understanding of war that dominates conventional Strategic Studies, anthropologists have long stressed the human impulse to find meaning in war, and stressed the cultural dimension of violence – its idiom, discourse and meaning.[26] In other words, the desire among mainstream social scientists to understand violence in utilitarian, instrumentally rational terms precludes consideration of what violence says and thinking of violence (including war) as 'a changing form of interaction and communication, as a historically developed form of *meaningful* action'.[27] Anthropological work also stresses a view of humans as 'historical and culture-bearing social beings' for whom relations of meaning-creation and symbolism are central.[28] Social 'reality', in other words, is constructed through the meaning that human beings impart to it.

Few practices or events touch with such poignancy issues of life and death as war does, and rationalising war is always a central concern for decision-makers. War is a phenomenon complex enough to generate imaginative thinking by participants, protagonists and bystanders alike. The notion of metaphor constitutes a central tool in understanding the way in which war was rationalised by liberal states in the first decade of the twenty-first century. The narrative of *policing war*, I argue, entailed the imagination of war 'as' policing, *in metaphorical terms*.

The word 'metaphor' comes from the Greek *metaphora* which literally means 'a carrying over'; etymologically, it comes from *meta*, 'over, across' + *pherein*, 'to carry, bear'.[29] According to the common view of metaphor as a linguistic phenomenon (sometimes described as the 'comparison theory' of metaphor), metaphors are matters of language only, not of thought or action. In this view, metaphor is of little consequence beyond being 'ornamental', a way of 'prettying up' speech or text. Juxtaposed with the linguistic view of metaphor is what George Lakoff and Mark Johnson call a cognitive view of metaphor.[30] In this view, metaphors are not simply stylistic devices: instead 'our conceptual system that is largely metaphorical ... the way we think, what we experience and what we do every day is very much a matter of metaphor'.[31] Thus 'metaphor' means precisely metaphorical concept, and a theory of metaphor is consequently as much a theory of the human conceptual system as a theory 'simply' of metaphor. This is not to say that metaphor as a feature of language should be ignored altogether, but rather that linguistic metaphors are derived from pre-existing conceptual ones rather than the other way round. Thus, 'the essence of metaphor is understanding and experiencing one kind of thing in terms of another'; in other words, *we think metaphorically because we need to.*[32] It is in this way that war has been rationalised by liberal states as *policing war*: by one abstract concept (war) is understood and experienced via another (policing). Emphasising the cognitive or conceptual view of metaphor entails recognition that the two concepts involved in a metaphor (in our case 'war' and 'policing') impose meaning on one another; they are 'active together' to produce a new meaning.[33]

The notion of metaphorical thinking contrasts with rationalist, empiricist thought, as traditionally understood. Unsuprisingly, 'metaphor' was explicitly shunned in seventeenth-century Cartesian thought.[34] Yet, a different light is shed on the demarcation between rationalist and post-rationalist attitudes to metaphor and metaphorical reasoning if we consider the understanding of metaphor in cognitive terms: metaphor, as Giambattista Vico tells us, 'is neither abuse nor folly, but the necessary means ... by which meaning is produced in a specific historical context. (...) Metaphor is thus not a rhetorical ornament, but a constitutive part of thought and society.'[35] Conventional readings of rationalist thought tend to overlook its figurative aspects, and, by the same token, miss the way in which cognitive metaphors take hold also in empiricist thought. In his compelling study *Cosmopolis: The Hidden Agenda of Modernity*, Stephen Toulmin offers an alternative to the standard reading of the origins of modernity, including the basic tenets of modern existence – the 'twin myths of 'rational' Modernity and 'modern' Rationality'.[36] The supposed (dis) connect between 'metaphor', 'rationality' and 'reason' is central to the conventional narrative of the modern period; a dichotomy between truth/reason on the one hand and art/imagination/subjectivism on the other reinforced also by the Romantics. For Toulmin, however, humility and scepticism did indeed have a place in modern thought and, like other periods, the modern era rested in part on the creation of myth. Ultimately, there is nothing specifically post-rationalist about metaphor: metaphorical processes are inextricably linked to human reason, and at that, 'not only reasoning about the world but also reasoning about the way that we reason'.[37]

Efforts have been made to use the idea of conceptual metaphor as an in-road into the study of international politics and war: Clifford Geertz suggested in his *The Interpretation of Cultures* that metaphors 'engender political power', and for this reason they can also be instruments of political change; and Paul Chilton refers to 'the policy-making mind' as being influenced by metaphor.[38] Similarly,

Roland Paris has illustrated how historical analogies are more than simple, rhetorical analogies: metaphorically, they structure ideas of what war actually *are*.[39] Political leaders are certainly enlivened by the idea that their actions need to be perceived as 'legitimate' and as a consequence resort to various 'sites of legitimation' – legal, moral, ethical.[40] Throughout history those fighting have nurtured and proclaimed ideal notions about what war *ought* to be, ideas that in turn influence their idea of what war *is* and their actual conduct in war.[41] The conceptual metaphor of 'policing' works as precisely such a legitimating device: it serves to legitimate the war-fighting of one warring party – the 'policing' party – vis-à-vis the 'criminal'/'terrorist' other. The rationalisation of *policing wars* involves recourse to a metaphor of some complexity and malleability, as we shall see.

The existence of long-standing traditions of moral and legal reasoning about war illustrates that the idea of conceiving certain acts (or actors) in war as immoral, illegitimate or criminal – constitutive elements of the *policing war* narrative – is far from new. Such narratives have impacted on thinking about what war is or ought to be for centuries; they form the essential background to what some refer to as a 'normative devaluation of war in the West'.[42] Describing the legal and moral traditions of curbing the excesses of war as a 'normative devaluation', however, only gives us part of the picture – it tells the story of how the authors of the ostensible normative devaluation understand, value and rationalise *their own* war-fighting in relation to that of others. Indeed, the illegality of targeting civilians in war, for instance, stands as a core principle of international law; yet states continue to laborate with the risks involved in warfare in ways that may encroach on this principle, for instance, by seeking to avoid deaths among their own soldiers and thus further endangering the lives of civilians or non-combatants. Martin Shaw characterises this as a logic of 'risk-transfer warfare', whereby the killing of civilians is 'by definition "accidental"'.[43] (This type of reasoning has become increasingly common with the rise in drone warfare: notably, the US military counts all adult males killed in drone strikes as 'militants' unless these individuals are specifically exonerated after their death.[44]) The appeal and currency of the policing metaphor lies in its affinity with the broader 'legalisation' of international relations and the claim that war is waged in the interest of upholding a certain order internationally.[45] This legalisation, I will argue, is a highly political project. Carl Schmitt's critique of the post-Versailles political order helps shed light also on the limits of the contemporary narrative of *policing war* – a strand that will be explored in Chapter 5.[46]

In order to make sense of the resort to metaphorical thinking about war, and heed the insight that those metaphors are culture-bound, we need to take seriously the categories that shape social and political thought in the largest sense. Unravelling the social embed-dedness of a specific understanding of war requires us to consider what fundamental ideas about societal life shape ideas about war. We need to unpack, in Stephen Toulmin's terms, the *intellectual scaffolding* of our time.

## War as socially embedded and the structure of this book

In *Cosmopolis,* Toulmin suggests that each period possesses an 'intel-lectual scaffolding' that underpins thoughts, beliefs and shared prac-tices.[47] Of the modern period, he writes:

> the image of *scaffolding* ... serves to remind us that, scientifically, the modern framework was suggestive, not directive. It defined possible lines for future work, it did not impose them by *fiat*. ... the world picture repeatedly changed shape in ways different from those foreseen in its original form ... As a result, modern science outgrew its framework, with scandalous results, and respectable opinion struggled to maintain the scaffolding intact, while remov-ing its individual timbers one by one.[48]

The quote from Toulmin is worth reciting at length for it tells us something particular about the approach he takes in uncovering the factors that shaped the early modern period and how their constant evolution and interplay was itself a key factor in shaping the mod-ern era. The image of intellectual scaffolding is particularly apposite: in the same way that a building under construction is surrounded by the scaffolding that will ensure its future completion, we might visualise the centrality of certain core ideas to the construction of any worldview or sense of being. A given example is the Cartesian dichotomy of the early modern imagination entailed the separation of Humanity from Nature, prompting series of other dichotomies 'endemic' to the modern period: reasons *vs* causes, mental *vs* material, actions *vs* phenomena and so on.[49] It is the scaffolding, rather than the building itself, that Toulmin encourages us to focus on, for while a building may stand securely once erected, its scaffolding is easily dismantled and appropriately vulnerable: the 'individual timbers [of scaffolding] may be removed one by one'.[50] The superseding or crowding out of one set of ideas by another also hints at what Toulmin calls the 'subtexts' of any given era – subtexts that expose the *reasons that certain ideas catch on at the time they do*.[51] By allowing for the imagination of an intellectual scaffolding, sustained by various subtexts, we are able to glimpse at a meta-level the kinds of changes that effect a collective imagination. Such collective imagination runs from the vast and fundamental notions of Being and history, to the imagination of 'discrete' events and practices such as war.

Charles Taylor takes an analogous approach via his notion of 'social imaginaries', which he explains as the 'way people imagine their social existence, how they fit together with others, how things go on between them and their fellows, the expectations that are normally met, and the deeper normative notions and images that underlie these expectations'.[52] Such imaginaries are just as often expressed in images, stories or legends; and acknowledge no difference between what is 'factual' and what is 'normative'. An understanding of the social imaginaries on which we rely is *more* than simply a background explanation for social practices or institutions; it makes for a fuller and wider 'grasp of our whole predicament'.[53] Similar ambitions have prompted others to refer to 'changes in the cultural self-image of the age, the models by which a society interprets itself' to describe the essence of debates about transition between eras – in this case between modernity and postmodernity.[54]

How then did what I call the metaphorical understanding of war 'as' policing – the rationalisation of *policing wars* – emerge? What subtexts underpin and sustain this imagination of war? What are the ideas that make up the 'intellectual scaffolding' for the contemporary liberal world, and how have they translated this particular ideal or preconception about war? These are the kinds of questions this book sets out to answer. To structure inquiry into the emergence of the narrative of policing wars and the conceptual scaffolding upon which it rests, I draw on key themes of social theory and philosophy: conceptions of TIME, SPACE, POWER and AGENCY. Together these dimensions hint at a fuller social structure upon which conceptions of 'meaning' in social and political life are built. There is, in other words, a *temporality* to all understandings of the world and political life; there is a *spatiality* to all understandings of the world and political life; there are implicit *readings of power* implicit in all worldviews; and there are specific views of *human relations and human agency* embedded too.

To open the analysis and provide essential background to the interventions in Afghanistan and Iraq, **Chapter 1** examines the 'explanations' of conflict that dominated mainstream academic debate during the 1990s, and the effect these theories came to have on the policy world of liberal internationalism. These narratives foreground the stories told about the wars in Afghanistan and Iraq, and reveal the extent of (perhaps unexpected) continuity between pre- and post-9/11 thinking about war. **Chapter 2** considers conceptualisations of time and temporality, and how they have impacted on recent decades' understanding of war in the Western world. Focusing on how conceptions of time has structured social thought and thus also our understanding of social practices, including war, allows us to explain, *inter alia*, why the policing wars of the twenty-first century appear endless. **Chapter 3** explores the dimension of space and asks what understandings of political spatiality are embedded in the narrative of policing war. It is argued herein that one of the most salient features of the policing war logic is its testimony to a depoliticised understanding of conflict and war, and that this in part can be traced to altered notions of spatiality. **Chapter 4** considers the theme of power, asking what conceptions of power underpin the contemporary rationalisation of policing wars, in counterinsurgency jargon tasked with 'transferring authority' from intervening forces to local ones in Afghanistan and Iraq. This discussion exposes the ways in which acknowledgement of real political conflict is elided through ubiquitous notions of power. **Chapter 5** draws together the themes of liberalism, internationalism and the notion of war 'without antagonism' that constitute undercurrents in the book as a whole.

By referring to war as the 'father and king of all', Heraclitus implored us to ask what has become of us as the world continues to be defined by war.[55] Unravelling *policing wars* entails unpacking an idealisation of war that essentially negates what Clausewitz found to be war's defining feature – coercion. In the narrative of policing war, the essentially coercive nature of war is obscured. War by liberal states is rationalised not as war proper but as a necessary corrective to disorder – a fantasy that has proved extraordinarily lasting in the liberal imagination. If we are to understand its most recent incarnation in the liberal discourse of the wars in Afghanistan and Iraq, we must look for the most fundamental reasons for its tenacity and uncover the way in which that narrative came to be socially embedded. This way of explaining the incidence of war starts from the assumption that war always reflects the societies that wage them, and emphasises the ways in which ideas about what war *is* interacts with much broader ideas about society, politics and the self.

# 1
# Narratives of Disorder

## Introduction: re-ordering conflict research

Conflict research was in vogue during the 1990s as theorists grappled with new global realities after the end of the Cold War, including the dissolution of the Soviet Union and global bipolarity. While Francis Fukuyama's thesis of an 'end of history' was widely contested, it certainly seemed that ideology – which had so busied people during the Cold War – occupied a less prominent role in explaining conflict following the fall of the Berlin Wall than it had in the decades prior. The demise of superpower rivalry was followed by widespread assumptions about a growing international liberal consensus; to those so minded, the post-Cold War world offered unprecedented promise for more peaceful relations both between and within states. It was this mood that then Secretary-General of the United Nations, Boutros-Boutros Ghali, captured when he in 1992 declared that 'the nations and peoples of the United Nations are fortunate in a way that those of the League of Nations were not. *We have been given a second chance to create the world of our Charter that they were denied.*'[1] Optimism about the prospects for a new international order was by no means confined to discussions within the UN, however; then US President Bill Clinton uttered similar hopes at the time of the signing of the Bosnia–Croat peace agreement in 1994.[2] The most paradigmatic statement is probably that given by Tony Blair, two years into his period as UK Prime Minister, in a speech at the Economic Club in Chicago in 1999: Blair proclaimed prospects for international order under the banner that 'we are all internationalists now'.[3]

17

Yet for all such proclamations, war, of course, persisted during the 1990s. And as images of death and destruction in Somalia, Rwanda and Bosnia were brought to Western audiences they stood in stark contrast to the visions of a 'new world order'. In the context of wilful optimism about the international community's capacity to create peace, it is perhaps not surprising that efforts to explain war came to centre on the question of whether armed conflict after the end of the Cold War was somehow of a different nature or new order than war previously. Inter-state conflict as it was conventionally known, after all, seemed to be in decline.[4] Mary Kaldor's concept of 'new wars' is archetypal in its amalgamation of many of the features that were highlighted in the conflict literature at the time: the effects of 'globalisation' (however defined); new practices and modes of warfare, including the increasing use of private force; and the prominence of particularist identity politics and other factors perceived to challenge the Westphalian model of state-on-state violence. All of these factors were included under a single label of purported 'newness'.[5] While Kaldor's thesis spawned much criticism (notably for being ahistorical), the pivotal position it came to occupy in debates about the causes and dynamics of conflict testifies to a widespread sentiment during the 1990s that existing understandings of war were somehow inadequate.[6] As this chapter will show, the assumption that there was something qualitatively different or new about war and conflict in the post-Cold War period was in itself closely bound up with the idea of a new apotheosis in the international community's quest to limit war and violence. The surge in optimism about a new world order, in other words, only made sense if the wars to be extinguished were understood to be of a particular kind: namely, wars amenable to external intervention. The exceptions to this assumption were few and far between, as reflected in Edward Luttwak's 1999 bizarrely entitled article 'Give war a chance'.[7]

Interest in conflict 'management' and 'resolution' grew tremendously during the 1990s, both as fields of academic research and in policy circles, and served to strengthen the internationalist and interventionist impulse among liberal decision-makers. The view of conflict as amenable to external intervention stemmed from particular view about the nature, causes and dynamics of conflict itself; motifs that in turn foregrounded the emergence of the imagination of policing war. Yet, despite strong voices in the West advocating external intervention in conflict, Western forces were seldom involved themselves: this was the era of growth in South-to-South peacekeeping.[8]

## Four narratives of (non-Western) war

Within the flurry of debate on the causes and dynamics of war during the 1990s, four strands can be identified as particularly influential in Western policy circles: first, the account of conflict as the breakdown or collapse of order and 'normal' political relations, often centred on the failure of the state; second, the depiction of armed conflicts as the unavoidable result of innate characteristics – a barbaric disposition, the clash between incompatible ethnic communities, civilisations and so on; and third, the understanding of conflict as essentially criminal in nature. Fourth, I turn to the more recent preoccupation with terrorism, and its particular impact on policy responses to conflict. All four narratives, as we shall see, are founded on the idea that war and war-fighting in developing states are somehow of a different *kind* from that of Western states – an essential differentiation that was to emerge as a key marker of liberal states' imagination of their own military ventures as *policing wars*.

### Conflict as the collapse of politics: war and state failure

In a widely cited article in *Foreign Policy* in 1992, Gerald B. Helman, former US ambassador to the UN in Geneva, and Steven R. Ratner, a former legal advisor to the US State Department and fellow at the Council on Foreign Relations, placed the issue of state failure firmly on the policy agenda. In their words, 'from Haiti in the Western Hemisphere to the remnants of Yugoslavia in Europe, from Somalia, Sudan, and Liberia in Africa to Cambodia in Southeast Asia, a disturbing new phenomenon is emerging: the failed nation-state, utterly incapable of sustaining itself as a member of the international community'.[9] A wide debate on 'failed' or 'collapsed' states ensued, primarily among IR and political theorists. For I. William Zartman, whose 1995 edited volume *Collapsed States: The Disintegration and Restoration of Legitimate Authority* was one of the most frequently cited on this topic, 'state collapse' refers to 'a situation where the structure, authority (legitimate power), law, and political order have fallen apart and must be reconstructed in some form, old or new. (...) Order and power (but not necessarily legitimacy) fall down to local groups and are up for grabs.'[10] Described as 'modern debellatios', the failed or collapsed states were predicted to be on the path of inevitable descent into 'violence and anarchy'.[11]

The notion of state failure had a tremendous impact on understandings of war in that period, and was invoked to shed light on both the causes and dynamics of conflict. Much of the literature points to a purportedly inevitable link between state collapse or failure and the incidence of violent conflict; Helman and Ratner posit this 'inevitability' as a consequence of decolonisation, which, they argue, resulted in the establishment of states that were in fact unable to function as independent entities.[12] Others hinged their analysis of war in the failed state on the presence of 'warlords', entrepreneurs of violence – sometimes understood as acquiring prominence as a consequence of state collapse, and sometimes as being the agents of state collapse in the first place.[13] In any event, the warlord persona that figured so prominently in the failed states literature of the 1990s contributed to the understanding of war as generally anarchic; in Roland Marchal's words, the term itself served to summarise 'a shared perception of a brutal and non-political figure' as the agent of war in the failed state.[14]

The claim about the inevitability of conflict in failed states is manifestly problematic. First, the diagnosis of a state as 'failed' constitutes an attempt to capture a set of very complex conditions and processes under a single label. The apparition of a condition of complete 'collapse' is contingent on a particular, preconceived, notion of what constitutes order and normality. To take but one example: Ken Menkhaus points out in his discussion of the literature on Somalia in the 1990s (the archetypal failed state) that conventional understandings overlook many important aspects of Somali societal structure. Thus, the rule of law in Somalia was never associated with a formal judiciary and police; instead, order was a reflection of local contracts between individuals and local sheik leaders (a pattern that is recognisable in other parts of the world, including Afghanistan).[15] Similarly, indifference to the external relationships of the ostensibly failed state and its position in the international system may lead to a naively decontextualised and ahistorical view both of the states in question and their violent conflicts.

Second, the particular understanding of war presented in much of the failed states thesis is problematic in its emphasis on uncontrollability, anarchy and relentless power-grabbing with little concern for 'politics' beyond a pursuit of power. Again, the Somali context is instructive: the description of state collapse in Somalia as a long and complex degenerative disease, leaving behind 'little but the wreckage of distorted traditions and artificial institutions, a vacuum that the most ruthless elements in that society soon filled', is illustrative of a depoliticised understanding of war.[16] The framing of conflict-affected states as 'failed' essentially amounted to a discourse of pathologisation, where the domestic populations was described as fundamentally dysfunctional while external or intervening forces were posited as functional.[17] In terms of understanding violence and war, the view of conflict simply as degeneration leaves precious little room for understanding the political content of conflict, its meaning or function for those involved. When Chris Hedges describes contemporary conflicts as 'Hobbesian playgrounds' pitting all against all, he pandered to just such views.[18]

Two impetuses appear to have shaped the dominant interpretations of the 'failed state' in the 1990s: a residual worldview shaped by the notion that winning is the sole object of war, and the assertion that a state is essential for the existence of a rule of law. The literature that coalesced around state collapse or failure shared the assumption that politics in the context of war and violence is necessarily tied to the state as the site of political encounters (a topic we will return to in Chapters 3 and 4). Accordingly, conflicts wherein the state's role was obscured or the state bypassed altogether – not being the immediate object of contention in the conflict – were susceptible to a depoliticised interpretation; and conflicts that were not amenable to a state-centred analysis were considered degenerative and anarchic.

The notion of the failed state finding a proper place in an ordered and regularised international society stood out as utterly implausible in these accounts. Nor were the conflicts of a failed state taken to be serious or legitimate contests – they were, after all, the product of failure and breakdown. Helman and Ratner regarded the idea of the failed state as an actor in its own right as utterly unfeasible; instead they located the conceptual basis for any effort on the part of the international community in engaging with the failed states, or its wars, in the idea of 'conservatorship'.[19] Typically, analogies were made with disorder within the domestic setting, where communities have responsibility for managing the affairs of persons 'utterly incapable of functioning on their own', placing the 'hapless individual under the responsibility of a trustee or guardian'.[20] The 'failed' epithet in this instance was unambiguous: with the societal malaise – whether the lone fool in the domestic setting or the collapsed, failed and utterly conflict-prone state in the international system – there could be no equal engagement.

While the debate about 'failed' and 'collapsed' states was a quintessentially 1990s one, it was given new licence in the post 9/11 context. However, the language changed after 9/11: we currently hear less about state 'collapse' than about 'weak states', state 'fragility', or, more vaguely, a 'lack of legitimate governance' as both a cause and consequence of conflict.[21] Tangential to the interpretation of conflict as collapse are narratives positing war as the result of innate hostility among human beings. In their emphasis on 'unreason' and 'chaos' such interpretations shared many of the assumptions of failed states literature.

### Nature and culture: notions of inevitable conflict

Robert Kaplan, an American journalist and travel writer, came to exert considerable influence on thinking about war and conflicts, particularly in the US military establishment. In his 1994 article, 'The coming anarchy', Kaplan focused on the troubled West African sub-region (and in other writings on the Balkans), but his analysis and predictions were endowed with much wider purchase.[22] For Kaplan Sierra Leone was a microcosm of what was taking place, albeit in a more tempered manner, throughout West Africa and much of the underdeveloped world: 'the withering away of central governments, the rise of tribal and regional domains, the unchecked spread of disease, and the growing pervasiveness of war'.[23] Combining Malthusian theory and essentialist identity claims, Kaplan painted an image of war transformed, where conflicts take the shape of 'a rundown, crowded planet of skinhead Cossacks and juju warriors, influenced by the worst refuse of Western pop culture and ancient tribal hatreds, and battling over scraps of overused earth in guerrilla conflicts that ripple across continents'; Kaplan went so far as to write of 'reprimitised man'. He found population growth, environmental degradation and 'cultural and racial clash' to be deeply related, and wrote ominously of what the next fifty years would behold: 'now the threat is more elemental: *nature unchecked*'.[24]

Interesting in this regard is how the pairing of environmental anxieties with the incidence of armed conflict undoubtedly fed into a view that de-emphasised agency on the part of the participants in contemporary wars. As Kaplan tells us of the 'geographic destiny' of certain parts of the world (the underdeveloped and overpopulated), his analysis is unmistakably determinist. Kaplan finds politics obliterated by the impact of natural resource depletion, overpopulation and ancient tribal/ethnic hatreds (where loyalty is not with political causes but with small units such as the immediate family or guerrilla commander). He claims that the 1990s are in this instance analogous with the period of the Thirty Years' War: 'Back then (...) there was no "politics" as we have come to understand the term, just as there is less and less "politics" today in Liberia, Sierra Leone, Somalia, Sri Lanka, the Balkans, and the Caucasus, amongst other places.'[25] The link between environmental degradation and the incidence of war was emphasised also in work of Thomas Homer-Dixon; and the Kaplan and Homer-Dixon theses have been shorthanded as theses of 'a new barbarism', the essence of which was nothing other than biocultural determinism.[26]

While Kaplan's single-handed influence should not be overstated, his views on identity and war in particular were echoed by a wide constituency of theorists concerned with the 'ethnic conflicts' of the 1990s (the Balkans, Rwanda and the former Soviet Union). Primordialist interpretations of ethnic belonging and resultant conflict gained ground during the 1990s; for instance, the interpretation of conflicts as the inevitable result of 'ancient hatreds' was frequently invoked by the Clinton administration at the time of the war in Bosnia.[27] Similar primodialist thinking could be found elsewhere too: Anatol Lieven has written of the dominance of essentialist views in Russian academic writings at the time, wherein blood, speech and custom were seen to have organic cohesion in the form of the *ethnos*, a distinct ethnic population. This interpretation was used, for instance, to mobilise support for the Russian war effort against the Chechen 'bandits'.[28] A common view among the 'ethnic conflict' theorists was that while the bipolar structure had dominated strategic interaction during the Cold War, it had merely kept a lid on 'simmering ethnic hatreds'. This imagery of a 'bubbling cauldron' containing deep-rooted animosities that went back hundreds, perhaps thousands, of years was repeated *ad nauseam* in this period in the news media and in academic research as people struggled to make sense of the fact that brutal wars were occurring in the very midst of the purported 'new world order'.[29]

Samuel P. Huntington's 1993 article in *Foreign Affairs*, 'The Clash of Civilizations?', prompted more debate than anything else the journal had published since the 1940s.[30] In Huntington's view, it was not nationality or ethnicity that was the most discriminatory and divisive; rather it was 'civilisations'. While he admits that the essence of a particular 'civilisation' is not easily unravelled, Huntington is clear that he finds religion to be a central defining characteristic: 'a person can be half-French and half-Arab and simultaneously even a citizen of two countries. It is more difficult to be half-Catholic and half-Muslim.'[31] When his sequel book was published in 1996 Huntington had dispensed with the question mark at the end of the title, and presented a stark image of perpetually conflicting civilisations. Huntington finds civilisational belonging to be basic and endemic to human existence, enshrined over centuries, and thus impossible to erase or overturn.[32] That these ostensibly intrinsic differences will result in violent conflict is, for Huntington, unavoidable: 'differences in culture and religion *create* differences over policy issues, ranging from human rights to immigration to trade and commerce to the environment'.[33] His view of civilisational identity as unitary and unchanging places Huntington squarely in the determinist camp, 'in the conflict between civilisations, the question is not "Which side are you on?" but "What are you?"'[34]

From Kaplan's new barbarism to Huntington's civilisational thesis, a series of unapologetically deterministic theories of conflict emerged over the course of the 1990s and came to shape Western policy agendas to a significant extent. People were depicted as unable to wilfully change preferences since these are, to such a large degree, determined by basic 'identity'; and thus politics of any different order than that contained in realist power political struggle was ignored – effectively making for a civilisational realism. Yet, we know that identities are far from static: rather, they are conflicted, contested and mutable.[35] In the same way as realist theories of IR are criticised for being self-perpetuating, essentialist views of identity create the 'reality' they purport to describe. Policymakers confronted with elites drumming up and politicising ethnicity have in of course realised this, but, as we shall see, this has not necessarily prevented them from creating 'remedies' based on similar reification of primordial belonging. Both the 1995 Dayton Agreement for Peace in Bosnia and Herzegovina and the composition of the Coalition Provisional Authority in Iraq in 2003 suffered from making ethnic belonging the key element of political representation.

Theories of war as essentially criminal in nature emerged as a reaction against the primordialist theories of ethnic belonging – attempts to rescue the 'rationality' of the supposedly 'irrational' combatants described by primordialists. Nonetheless, theories of conflict as criminality that emerged in the policy-oriented conflict literature in the mid to late 1990s also, in the end, served to depoliticise understandings of 'non-Western' war among liberal policymakers in the period.

## The banalisation of war: conflict as criminality

Two distinct narratives of the post-Cold War period have contributed to this genre of conflict literature: the first captured by the so-called 'economic turn' in conflict analysis, when various authors began to devote more attention to the economic dynamics of war (most, but not all of it illicit); and the second in more generalised accounts of conflict as essentially criminal in nature. When World Bank economist Paul Collier wrote in 1999 that 'a useful conceptual distinction for understanding the motivation for civil war is that between greed and grievance', the phrase became a focal point within the conflict literature.[36] Collier and co-author Anke Hoeffler presented an analysis of the causes of conflict based on econometric analysis, where a large number of conflict cases were tested for the relative presence of measurable variables (proxies). To indicate 'greed' as a motivation for armed conflict, Collier and Hoeffler relied on three proxies: the availability of primary commodities ('lootables'), the proportion of young men in society, and the amount of education; for 'grievance' the degree of ethnic and religious fractionalisation, economic inequalities, (lack of) political rights and 'government economic incompetence' were selected.[37] Collier's conclusions pointed unequivocally in favour of the 'greed' thesis: for instance, countries dependent on primary commodity exports were found to stand a four times greater risk of falling into conflict than others. Conversely, education (a proxy for greed, oddly) reduced the risk of conflict, while political and economic inequalities had no effect at all on the propensity for conflict.[38]

Collier has been criticised on various methodological grounds, notably for conflating correlation with causation, and for his choice of 'proxies'. Critics have questioned the use of lack of education as a proxy for greed rather than grievance, and asking whether there were important factors omitted from both the greed and grievance calculations. Most importantly, however, Collier was criticised for his reliance on the classical economists' view of man as a rational, calculating and profit-maximising individual.[39] For Collier, the idea of inferring motivations from patterns of behaviour is uncontroversial: 'If someone says "I don't like chocolates" but keeps on eating them, we infer that she really does like chocolates, and the question of why she says otherwise is (…) relegated to being of secondary importance.'[40] For theorists concerned with social relations this reasoning, although it may uncover *a type* of truth, obscures relevant social, historical and contextual conditions that shape individual behaviour.[41]

For David Keen, highlighting the economic dynamics of conflict was in itself a way of affirming the 'rationality' of combatants. His restating of the Clausewitzian aphorism about war as 'the continuation of politics with an admixture of other means' into 'war as the continuation of economics by other means' portrayed local warring parties as equally the *Homo economicus* familiar from peaceful and well-off societies.[42] David Keen and Mats Berdal have made the case for distinguishing between 'political' and 'non-political' functions of violence, where 'political' violence was 'violence aimed at changing the rules of the game, emanating from the capital', while 'non-political' functions of violence were seen to incorporate three main types (economic functions, security functions and psychological functions).[43] It was described how, 'much of the violence cannot be easily explained as "political". Rather, it appears to have more local and immediate functions, often very economic.'[44] Characteristic of Berdal and Keen, however, was their careful emphasis on protracted conflicts (or 'complex emergencies' as they were often referred to at the time) being characterised by 'the interaction of political and economic agendas' rather than by one or the other on its own, producing 'alternative structures of power and profit'.[45] Karen Ballentine and Jake Sherman echoed this view by underlining in the sequel volume to *Greed and Grievance* that the conceptual distinction between the two presumed categories was of little practical relevance and, in itself, had had a stymieing effect on the debate.[46]

While the vast political economy literature fine-tuned and modified Collier's thesis, its original exposé left a significant mark on
the understandings of conflict in international policy circles, and
especially in World Bank circles.[47] The focus on methodological
individualism and economic man assumed war and violence to be
comprehensible through reliance on anonymous indicators and
measurable variables. The faith in quantification and the appealing
'clarity' of numerical results testifies to what Philip Windsor has
called the lure of positivist thought: while economic dynamics are
important in giving a complete image of war (especially its prolonga-
tion), they do not account for why these economic ambitions took
such violent expression.[48] Thus, since purely economic explanations
could not account for violence that 'shocked the moral conscience' of
Western observers (such as the maiming of civilians in Sierra Leone,
or the public display of dead American soldiers dragged through the
streets of Mogadishu in 1993) they contributed to the *non-explanation*
of violence as 'meaningless', 'barbaric' or simply 'evil'. This ignores
insights, in particular from anthropology, that tell us that violence is
very rarely 'meaningless' or 'senseless'.[49]

John Mueller's argument that contemporary conflicts are in fact
nothing but 'remnants of war', little more than 'policing problems', either for the domestic state or the international community
more broadly, is the quintessential 'war as criminality' argument.[50]
A cornerstone of Mueller's reasoning is his differentiation between
'criminal' and 'disciplined' warfare and between 'criminal' and
'disciplined' armies. Within his category of criminal armies, Mueller
finds two essential types: the 'mercenary' and the 'brigand' types,
exhibiting distinct types of organised violence.[51] As examples of the
former Mueller cites the 'thugs' (purportedly influenced by Rambo
films) perpetrating conflict in Croatia and Bosnia in the mid-1990s
where he asserts that 'what passed for "ethnic warfare" (...) seems
then to have been something far more banal: the creation of communities of criminal violence and predation'.[52] In support of his
view of fighters seeking violence for 'fun and profit', often under the
influence of alcohol Mueller cites accounts of the Rwandan conflict
and genocide, recounting how 'drunken militia bands, fortified with
assorted drugs from ransacked pharmacies, [moved] from massacre to
massacre'.[53] Groups found to be motivated and sustained simply by
'organized racketeering crime' involving predation, armed robbery,

marauding and so on are taken to represent the 'brigand approach' which, echoing Collier, Mueller finds to be more likely in countries that rely on primary commodity exports. Here Mueller includes conflicts as disparate as the ones in West Africa, Somalia, Colombia, Sudan, Angola, Congo, Burma, Central Asia and the Caucasus.[54]

While providing an elaborate list of potential reasons for people to fight (for fun and profit; narcosis; coercion; drill, discipline, leadership, submission to authority; honour, duty, glory; love and beliefs), Mueller returns to the difference he posits between 'criminal' and 'disciplined'. To Mueller the trajectory is clear: with the decline of the Cold War both international war and an 'important form of civil war', namely conflicts between disciplined or 'semi-disciplined' armies (here citing the later stages in Vietnam), also disappeared; '... so only criminal warfare remains'.[55] Mueller's thesis explicitly diminishes the fighters of contemporary conflicts: in support of his narrative of war in the late twentieth and early twenty-first century as essentially an activity of 'criminals' he considers that 'war has increasingly been reduced to its pathetic, if often highly destructive, remnants'.[56] He finds these 'criminal' forces to be lacking in organisation, discipline, popular support, ideological commitment and even courage.[57] Mueller's view of the dawn of a 'new era of remarkable consensus', where developed countries 'apply military force – that is, war – to police [these remnants of war]' aptly illustrates the absorption of the metaphorical understanding of war as policing.[58] The vehemental rejection of alternative views is evident in Mueller's cynicism about the people affected by the use of 'policing' force: 'the people whose lives are being saved don't know who they are, and are often critical or even contemptuous of their unappreciated saviours'.[59]

Despite the efforts to dispel primordialist readings of conflict from the minds of policymakers, later theorists' collective emphasis on economic motivations, greed and criminality did little to shift what had become a broader trend in the understanding of war 'elsewhere': the view that the war-fighting of 'non-Western' participants was somehow of a different kind. The view of conflict as essentially criminal – whether through individual petty crime or more organised resource exploitation – effected a seeming shift in the minds of policymakers devising responses to conflict, but in reality folded neatly within the proponents of a new world order's desire to understand the continued incidence of violent conflict as 'disorderly' – and thereby locating their own response as that of a 'corrective' or 'order-creating' force.

## Terrorism: more terrible than war?

While it was popular among authors who saw wars essentially as criminal in nature to declare the Clausewitzian aphorism of war as a continuation of politics by other means redundant, the focus on terrorism adds a further twist to the story of how war and conflict became narrated in the post-Cold War era. While most understandings of terrorism include the notion that indiscriminate violent acts are perpetrated for a political purpose, recent discourses on terrorism (or rather, terrorists) have had a profoundly depoliticising effect precisely on the understanding of war.[60] Thus we find another juncture in narratives of non-Western conflicts: the growing preoccupation with terrorism as a phenomenon 'distinct' from war.

In conflicts such as those in Northern Ireland, Israel–Palestine or Sri Lanka, the supposed duality between conflicts politically understood and terrorism has been a recurring theme. Nonetheless, the preoccupation with terrorism as a phenomenon in the context of war clearly increased post-9/11, opening up for a criminalisation and depoliticisation of warring parties and the conflicts as such. Conflicts in the North Caucasus, Uzbekistan, Thailand, the Philippines, Indonesia and Colombia, not to mention Iraq and Afghanistan, have been variously referred to as instances of terrorism rather than war or conflict.[61] Classic literature generally accepts that 'terrorism' is defined by the nature of the act, which may take place both in the context of war or in an otherwise peaceful setting.[62] Such a view does not necessarily generate any conclusions about the occurrence of terrorist acts signalling that the situation is no longer a case of 'war' but instead a case of terrorism and counter-terrorism – an essential part of the policing metaphor. More recently, 'new terrorism' scholars commonly point to four features that ostensibly make terrorism today distinct and 'new': the transnational and loose network organisation of perpetrators of terrorism; a deeply religious motivation for carrying out terrorist attacks; even more indiscriminate targeting than previous or 'old' terrorism; and a desire to maximise destruction and killing.[63] The characterisation of contemporary terrorism offered by the 'new terrorism' scholars is difficult to reconcile with conflict as traditionally understood – as a political phenomenon, with a focus on control of the state. Instead, interpretations of 'new terrorism' have generated a view of conflict akin to the one described by Kaplan and others a decade earlier, where violence is conceived as largely irrational, fanatical and utterly irredeemable.

This understanding paints a crude image of pathological individuals and groups, invoking the trope of the 'barbarian' with whom political engagement is unthinkable.[64] The pathologisation of certain actors is underlined by the increasing currency of psychological profiling of terrorists (something which, incidentally, appears to go against the recognised insight that evil can indeed be perpetrated by 'ordinary men'), and plays up to the demonisation of certain groups in war.[65] Writing of the Chechen conflict, Julie Wilhelmsen demonstrates how the creation and bolstering of distinct enemy images (the Russian's image of the Chechen 'bandit' and later 'Islamic terrorist') contributed to changing the dynamics of the conflict itself, drastically lessening the prospects for political engagement with Chechen insurgents, and increased unrest in the wider North Caucasus.[66] To call an adversary 'terrorist' is a clear signal that they are not officially regarded as political counterparts, which is precisely the function of 'naming terrorists': a process that only fairly recently was institutionalised through official lists that 'proscribe' or 'designate' organisations and individuals as 'international terrorists', such as by the US, the UK and the European Union (EU).[67]

Proscription is a fairly recent practice: in the UK, it was first introduced in 1974 by the Foreign Office but then referring exclusively to Northern Ireland. The UK list was expanded in 2001 to cover 'international terrorist organisations'. At the US State Department the practice of listing 'international terrorist organisations' was introduced in the mid-1990s; whereas the EU established its list in December 2001. Since 2001 the UN Security Council maintains a list of organisations 'affiliated with al-Q'aeda and the Taliban', rather than 'international terrorist organisations' per se – a notable difference.[68] Given the preoccupation with al-Q'aeda and 'catastrophic' terrorism in the years following 9/11, and the extent to which this influenced the interpretation also of conflicts where al-Q'aeda in fact was not involved, the practice by governments and international organisations of 'proscribing' terrorist organisations is perhaps unsurprising. However, it also fits well with the broader trajectory of conflict analysis since the end of the Cold War in its downplaying of political content, its emphasis on 'un-reason', chaos and a return to 'barbarism'.

Several themes emerge from the debates that took root during the 1990s about the causes and dynamics of conflict: an emphasis on unreason, chaos and irrationality on the part of fighters; the downplaying of agency in the context of war; and the general notion of wars lacking a political purpose. Together they fed into a widespread view that 'political legitimacy' (in Mary Kaldor's words) was disappearing from war.[69] Such narratives of disorder in turn became coupled with the idea of international responses as the (re)creation of order.

## Narratives of disorder and the (re)creation of order

'Given that states cannot fight other "states like us" they increasingly see their enemies as different in organisation and rationality,' wrote Mikkel V. Rasmussen of Western understandings of war a few years after 9/11.[70] While the understanding of war as the disintegration of politics was based on reliance on narrow understandings of rationality, whereby it only seemed 'rational' to engage in war if the object was to secure control over the state, Rasmussen's statement highlights the pervasiveness of the shift in perception of 'Western' versus 'non-Western' war. Moreover, a limited understanding of 'rationality' in the context of war displaced consideration of agency in the sense of deliberate will on the part of those engaged in violent struggle and war. For those who understood war as essentially criminal in nature, the protagonists of war no longer sought to accomplish goals beyond their own narrow purposes – this was what enabled theorists like Mueller to arrive at a view of conflict as 'pathetic'. And while the view of conflict as criminality can be seen to trivialise war, the (re)interpretation of war under the terrorism-lens, conversely, dramatised war to the extent that it seemed apocalyptic, out-of-this-world and, again, ultimately apolitical.

### Responding to disorder

British diplomat Robert Cooper was among those who seized on the failed states thesis as guidance for international policy.[71] To bring war to a conclusive end, the argument went, what was needed was a rebuilding of the state through the establishment of functioning state institutions. This in turn would enable political relations both between and within states (a topic to which we will return in Chapter 3).[72] Responses to state failure have been given overwhelming attention in international debates about war and have spawned a host of different policy incarnations: from 'capacity-building', security sector reform (SSR) and 'stabilisation' to the broader concept of 'peacebuilding'.[73] The term 'peacebuilding' was introduced by then UN Secretary General Boutros-Boutros Ghali in 1992, defined as 'action to identify and support structures which tend to strengthen and solidify peace to avoid a relapse into conflict'.[74] In this way, the general concern with state failure or collapse led external actors to strive to create a new type of order in domestic societies, generally through the establishment of state institutions (notably police, military and judiciary).

So too were theories of war as the result of primordial hatred associated with the ambition on the part of external actors to (re)create order. The focus this time was on the equal representation of different groups, ethnically or otherwise defined. David Campbell in his *National Deconstruction: Violence, Identity and Justice in Bosnia* (1996) convincingly demonstrated how the 'ethnic conflict' paradigm for understanding conflict translated into interventionist policies that in fact prompted the *reproduction* of ethnic faultlines as interveners bought into particularist claims about the primacy of ethnic belonging for political organisation.[75] In this way, a particular problematisation (of Bosnia) demanded a particular 'solution', making 'Bosnia' possible only through partition.[76] Unsurprisingly, primordialist theories of ethnic belonging as an explanation of conflict generated strategies that *reified* the politicisation of ethnicity and failed to encourage nonnationalist forms of social and political life. Walter Posch has similarly showed how the international community's fixation on ethnic identity in post-Saddam Hussein Iraq has become self-fulfilling: 'it appears that tripartite Iraq has become a reality and the very framework in which political discourse takes place...'[77]

The narrative of war as criminality produced yet another variant of 'responding to disorder'. International institutions (as well as individual states) were pushed to develop strategies specifically targeting the economic dimensions of conflict.[78] As Mats Berdal pointed out, the readiness with which policymakers absorbed narratives emphasising the economic dynamics of conflict ought not surprise us as 'the reduction of a conflict to a struggle over economic resources also reduced, at least in theory, the policy challenge'.[79] In this way, an interest in the (re)establishment of order translated a broad concern with the interrelationship between security and development into limited technical measures of 'managing conflict'. An example is the effort to deny combatants access to profitable illicit trade through technical measures that ultimately address the symptoms rather than causes of conflict.[80] The view of conflict as the petty pursuit of criminal motives, and thus thoroughly apolitical, conveniently displaces controversies over the international community's role when intervening in conflict.

Finally, the preoccupation with terrorism constitutes yet another variant of the view of war as disorder; it too has been endowed with a concomitant will to (re)establish order. The dominance of anti- or counter-terrorism policies of the international agenda in the years following can hardly be overstated: almost all recent major policy documents concerned with international security accord central importance to the issue of terrorism.[81] With the conflation of conflict and terrorism in narratives of international order, 'conflict management' and 'counter-terrorism' have been similarly conflated in recent years. The integration of counter-terrorism into the war repertoire has served to reinforce many of the 'order-creating' strategies mentioned hitherto: state-building/peacebuilding policies have been accredited with preventing terrorist violence (most recently under the term 'counterinsurgency', to be discussed in Chapter 4). Moreover, counter-terrorism has begun to be mainstreamed into international development policy, to the marked consternation of development scholars who believe that linking the two will ultimately do disservice both to the project of poverty reduction and the quest for global security.[82]

(Re)creating 'order' is no small matter; the view of conflict as disorder has led to remarkably far-reaching interventions on the part of the international community into states' domestic affairs. While the early calls for 'conservatorship' or 'trusteeship' as a response to the failed state were met with disdain, the successor concept of peacebuilding (invoked also to remedy social and political fragmentation, crime and terrorism) carried forth many of the same core ideas; above all, its scope was decidedly vast.[83] Yet, as the above discussion hints, the problems of responding to 'war as disorder' are fundamental, going beyond challenges of magnitude or legitimacy.

Mark Duffield thus criticises the linking of security and development agendas for leading not to the betterment of people's lives, but to the governing of those people, in fact maintaining the divide between development and underdevelopment.[84]

## Conclusion

The liberal internationalist/interventionist agenda (what James Mayall calls the 'new interventionism') established during the 1990s enjoyed far wider support than the 'war on terror'.[85] It is interesting therefore that the two frames are not as far apart as the 'war on terror' critics like to think: most markedly, perhaps, they are united by the idea of conflict as a-political (an issue to which we will return in Chapter 5.) A point that clearly emerges from the discussion in this chapter is the distinct view of external actors' use of military force as they intervene to 'restore order'. Intervening in the interest of 'restoring order', in turn ostensibly distinguishes this type of military activity from waging 'war'. The belief in the very possibility of such a distinction is an intrinsic part of the metaphorical view of war as policing that characterised the interventions in Afghanistan and Iraq.

# 2
# Perpetual Policing Wars

## Introduction: perpetual policing war

'As of the opening years of the twenty-first century, the mightiest, richest, best-equipped, best-trained armed forces that have ever existed are ... looking into an abyss.'[1] The abyss to which Martin Van Creveld refers in the opening to his book *The Changing Face of War* (2006) is the prospect of regular (state) forces locked in counter-insurgency wars wherein they are unable to prevail, yet at the same time cannot concede defeat. Thus Van Creveld raises the prospect of 'regular, state-owned armed forces being forever doomed to go on losing [wars]'.[2] John Mueller draws the same conclusion when he states: '"Decisive" is a military term and does not pertain to police work. Wars may end, but policing never does.'[3] The notion of 'policing' being logically 'perpetual', that is, perpetual by its very nature, will be explored in this chapter. Is Mueller is right to say that by metaphorically conceiving current wars as 'policing wars' the liberal world eschews any ability to end the wars it is fighting? This would appear to be an immediate conclusion from analogies between war and criminality and, by extension, war and policing. There are few aspirations to the use of policing as a means to putting a final end to criminality or disorder in society. Instead policing, in the domestic setting, is conceived as the means by which disorder is managed and kept to a minimum. What, may we ask, happens to war when it is conducted under such a logic? What, more profoundly, accounts for the seemingly contradictory impulse to think of war as perpetual policing?

Paradoxically, though Mueller is clear that 'wars end [but] policing never does', he is decidedly optimistic about the prospects for policing wars. Contra Van Creveld's assessment, Mueller remains convinced that regular forces would always eventually triumph against irregular ones.[4] Mueller's invoking (and endorsing) of the policing paradigm is contradictory because on the one hand he is certain that the West will prevail over its opponents ('a criminal or near-criminal force tends to be cowardly and incompetent when confronted by an effective disciplined one'), while on the other he rightly points out that the policing paradigm itself obliterates the prospect for a decisive ending or victory in war.[5] The ambiguity in Mueller's reasoning – that regular forces should prevail owing to their greater strength and capacity, yet at the same time cannot do so definitely because there cannot, by definition, be a decisive end to policing wars – neatly summarises the central *problématique* of this chapter: the paradox of perpetual policing war. Policing has no beginning and no end; it is directed at the maintenance of order. If this is such an impossible metaphor, what reasons can we find behind its apparent currency in recent years?

From a different horizon, David Keen describes the war on terror as an 'endless war' because in his understanding it is a war that the key actors (notably the US and the UK under the Bush and Blair administrations) *do [did] not necessarily want to win*.[6] For Keen the war on terror (and its actual wars in Afghanistan, Iraq and elsewhere) should be seen as 'a system conferring important benefits [on the parties waging it]', rather than a contest that either side seeks to conclusively end – a system, in Keen's view, dominated by financial and economic considerations.[7] He highlights a double-edged connection between 'endlessness' and war at the outset of his book: 'if the war on terror is an endless war in the sense of a perpetual war', Keen reasons, 'it does not appear to be an endless war in the sense that it lacks any goal or purpose.'[8] For Keen, the functions served by war, whether economic, political or psychological functions, *are* in fact its ends – a conceptual leap that is sustained throughout the book. Yet, outlining the hidden goals of the proponents of a war on terror fails to explain why such deception 'works' – the underlying reasons for such tenacity. What models, then, by which a society interprets itself (in Gerard Delanty's terms) underpin the discourse on war as an endless pursuit of criminal elements and the establishment of 'order'?

What elements of broader intellectual scaffolding, in other words, can be said to sustain the notion of endlessness or perpetuity?

The argument presented in this chapter is that war is becoming perpetual or endless quite simply because the liberal world is *unable to imagine conclusive endings* to the wars it is currently fighting. To substantiate this claim and offer some suggestion as to why this state of affairs has come about, an alternative reading is offered of how current practices of war – shaped by a metaphor of policing – relate to the notion of endlessness or perpetuity. The discussion is divided into three parts. In the first part, I consider the way in which notions of time or temporality are understood in what we might call the collective consciousness of the contemporary liberal world, drawing primarily on the work of social theorists Zaki Laïdi and Agnes Heller, and sociologist Zygmunt Bauman. I suggest here that endlessness or perpetuity itself is in fact a central element of a Western, liberal, 'postmodern' consciousness. In the second part of the chapter I argue that the motif of endlessness has been manifest in US and UK war-fighting in Afghanistan and Iraq, such that reference to the war on terror as the 'Long War' appears quite the understatement.[9] Three salient features of contemporary wars are discussed in order to substantiate the claim about the centrality of endlessness in war. The final part of the chapter highlights some of the implications and consequences of the difficulty in imagining an end to war.

## Time in the postmodern consciousness

The way in which a society makes sense of the relationship between past, present and future – the objectification of its place in history – is central to its collective consciousness. For Zygmunt Bauman the relationship between time and space is the most important part of understanding the specific quality of our time.[10] In Manuel Castells' words, space and time are the 'fundamental, material dimensions of human life'; and only by investigating these categories can we glimpse the structures of thought that condition our understanding of the world and ourselves.[11] So too for Kimberly Hutchings, assumptions about time 'fundamentally shape what we can and cannot know about world politics today'.[12] Indeed, a conceptualisation of time – not in the metaphysical sense, but as *durée* and historicity – can be seen as a prerequisite for the notion of a 'historical consciousness'.

Such is the centrality of our understanding of time, temporality and historicity that we ought not to be surprised by its importance in 'making sense' of war, a fundamentally social and human activity. To enable a meaningful discussion of the conceptions of time that animate the present collective consciousness, we do well to first give some consideration to the period from which it has emanated, that of classical modernity.

At least from the time of the Enlightenment, the view of history as fundamentally progressive has been central to the European collective imagination. Tradition and religiosity were cast aside in favour of faith in humans' capacity to realise Progress by virtue of their capacity for Reason; this was a central message from the *philosophes*. Thus, the early modern consciousness implied that people acquired an understanding of their age 'in terms of its being a product of world-historical progression, where each stage contained its own possibilities and limitations as well as being superseded in turn by another stage'.[13] Not that the displacement of God and the prominent role accorded to Reason should be understood simply as a result of scientific discoveries: it was as much a result of developments in the domain of moral philosophy. Indeed, the point of departure for Immanuel Kant, quintessential philosopher of the Enlightenment, is precisely in the tension between science and morality, or between *phenomena* and *noumena*.[14] In Kant's view, the freedom of will must be explained in relation to the natural world. The world of *phenomena*, in other words, is the world of things in their manifestation or appearance; what science can know. The world of *noumena*, by contrast, is the world of things as they are in themselves or 'as they might be known if knowledge of them could be had without the mediation of experience'.[15] We access the world of *noumena* through morality rather than science, Kant tells us, and it is here that we are free to be rational and autonomous agents, free from 'self-incurred immaturity'.[16] As Pierre Hassner's reading shows, the reconciliation of the realms of *phenomena* and *noumena* assures Kant's conception of history as fundamentally progressive, and of philosophy as pointing the direction of and giving hope for 'progress'.[17]

From the progressivist worldview that characterised the modern imagination we can discern a particular understanding of time and temporality: its linearity. Indeed, linearity or a linear understanding of time is contained in the very meaning of the term 'modern', which came to indicate something that had not existed previously. As John Gray shows, the adjacent idea that the future would be different from the past was an idea peculiar to the modern imagination.[18] The Greeks and the Romans, by contrast, had interpreted history in a cyclical manner, whereas Medieval Europeans saw history in an altogether different way, as 'a moral drama that concluded with the end of the world [with] the conditions of earthly life ... much as they always had been'.[19] In the Medieval imagination, in other words, life may be different in another geographical place but earthly life as such would remain essentially the same. The progressivist turn of the seventeenth and eighteenth centuries brought with it a sense that the future 'had been invented'; only thereafter, towards the end of the eighteenth century, did the idea of the future as the site of a better world catch on.[20]

Tellingly, Isaiah Berlin has described teleological thinking as 'a framework in which everything – or almost everything – was to be understood and described'.[21] In other words, the notion of telos provided unity and direction to collective imagination: a framework in which key features of the modern world, such as the emphasis on technological progress, could be 'rationally' understood. Means–ends rationality (instrumental rationality) was to become in Max Weber's words the 'operative principle' of the modern age, underpinning the central institutions and practices of the modern period including, most importantly, the rise of industrial capitalist society. Yet means–ends rationality did not signal just an instrumental pursuit of aims. As Zaki Laïdi points out, the teleological perspective entails a 'triple notion' of 'foundation, unity and final goal': foundation implies 'the basic principles on which a project depends'; unity the '"world images", collected into a coherent plan of the whole'; and final goal the 'projection towards an elsewhere that is deemed to be better'.[22] The trifold account of the teleological worldview offered by Laïdi thus highlights its existential implications; above all, the 'existence' of telos endowed modern imagination with a sense of meaning.[23] In other words, the distinctive way in which the modern age objectified its place in history – the linear way in which people would relate the past, the present and the future to one another – provides us with important clues as to how existential meaning hung together with an understanding of time itself (as *durée* and temporality).

This specific understanding of the present that characterised the modern imagination was that of transit from the past to the future.

As Heller tells us, the modernist progressivist worldview meant that 'being in the present' was the same as living in 'a transitory state, stage or world, compressed between the past and the future'.[24] In effect, the present ceased to have existential meaning in its own right and instead became a sort of 'accelerated projection toward the future'. Indeed, the modernist imagination '*marginalized the present* through the historical recollection of the past (as necessity) and through the project and projection of an infinite future (freedom)'.[25]

A consequence of the marginalisation of the present was the specific sense of self-awareness and identity it generated. In the modern imagination, man was in the present by virtue of the past and heading toward (a specific) future. Bauman similarly notes how 'being modern means being perpetually ahead of oneself, in a state of constant transgression (in Nietzsche's terms, one cannot be *Mensch* without being, or at least struggling to be, Übermensch); it also means having an identity which can exist only as an unfulfilled project'.[26] The present thus became the 'territory of human experiment and creation, ... forced to obey the human will'.[27] In the modern imagination, human beings could inflict their will on the present in the name of a utopian future. In other words, the 'present' became human agency and instrumental rationality instantiated with the prospect of a better future.

It was the notion of human beings' deliberate imposing of will on the world that led Friedrich Nietzsche to predict that the modern consciousness was to have a devastating impact on war.[28] The calamities of total war, the Holocaust and the atomic bombs dropped over Hiroshima and Nagasaki stand out as stark examples of how the present could be marginalised in the name of a desired future. For liberals and their critics alike, war in the twentieth century became 'more than just an instrument of policy; it became a medium of progress, social reengineering and political change'.[29] The step from social engineering to social experimentation proved all too short as conditions in the German Third Reich, the USSR, the DDR and elsewhere so graphically demonstrate. Summarily, it seemed possible in the modern era to squeeze the present into near insignificance by instrumentalising it and living instead *for* the future.

Regardless of whether 'postmodernity', 'second modernity', 'reflexive modernity' or 'liquid modernity' is the most appropriate conceptual label, many thinkers agree that there is something distinctive

Seems to conflate
modernity with liberalism!

about the present period. Jean-François Lyotard's view that an end to 'grand narratives' was wrought with the end of the Cold War has resonated widely: as the stand-off between two distinctively modern ideologies, liberalism and communism, came to an end, it no longer seemed possible to espouse ideologies with the same sense of predestination or unstinting faith as previously. Again, Zaki Laïdi explains this well:

> If the debate about the 'end of History' has any meaning, this is it. The crisis of expectation ... poses urgently, and in new terms, the problem of a *representation of the future that is not a goal-driven projection* in a preordained direction, with a predetermined outcome, of a potential future.[30]

The connection between the end of telos and the way in which the present, past and future, are related to one another in current discourses is significant in at least two ways. In the first instance, the collapse of teleological thinking rendered problematic the account of the modern imagination as fundamentally guided by instrumental rationality – a point to which I will return below. Second, the end of teleological thinking affected people's sense of existential meaning, their sense of purpose and direction. It is for this reason that Laïdi insists on the notion of crisis: the present crisis is a *crisis of meaning*, and as any crisis it is experienced existentially.[31] This brings significant consequences for how we understand historical and social conditions and change – including, as we shall see, our understanding of war.

For Zygmunt Bauman, the end of telos produced a wish for 'immediate, "on the spot" fulfilment – but also immediate exhaustion and fading of interest'.[32] For this reason, Bauman advises, we should think of ours as 'an era of instantaneity', wherein the present can no longer be marginalised in the interest of meaningful and utopian future. Bauman's claim is reminiscent of Agnes Heller's assessment of the present age that 'we (post) moderns are living in the *absolute present tense*'.[33] If the present can no longer be rationalised (or 'legitimised') in terms of a knowable future, it seems that the narrative ability to objectify the present time and its place in history is lost, or at least altered. As sociologists are fond of pointing out, the present has become a theme in and of itself. This theme recurs also in the work of Manuel Castells, who has argued that the contemporary period is distinct in that it sees the social organisation of space determining our conception of time, rather than the other way around.[34] Castells' argument is that the spatial organisation of the postmodern world (to which we shall return in detail in Chapter 3) is one where the production of instantaneous information through new communication technologies leads to 'a relentless effort to annihilate time'.[35] The result is a compression of time into *timeless* time. One might take this further to say that when time is no longer understood in a linear relational way, we lose not only the 'symbolic representation' of the future but also the symbolic representation of time itself.[36]

Though he does not invoke the term of crisis, Bauman's metaphor of liquids/fluids to characterise the postmodern condition points similarly to the existential implications of the decline of a teleological worldview contingent on fundamental 'truths'. For Bauman, the contemporary relationship with time (or to the present) is conditioned by the very structure of modern society, which is in radical transformation. The postmodern world is witnessing a change from a reliance on reassuringly solid concepts to more liquid ones (solids melted and dissolved), making ours a period of 'liquid modernity'.[37] Most importantly, Bauman tell us, the solids being melted are the 'bonds that interlock individual choices and collective projects and actions'.[38] In the absence of teleological thinking, the link between the individual's quest and the collective's has been severed or at least significantly weakened. Similarly, the way in which power operates has been affected by the transition into liquid times, Bauman tells us. Whereas modern power structures were aptly depicted by Michel Foucault's metaphor of a 'Panopticon', wherein the quintessential technique of power was that of total control and constant surveillance, power and its structures have also morphed into liquid shape.[39] Bauman identifies 'escape, slippage, elision and avoidance' as the prime techniques of contemporary power. Thus the exercise of power no longer pertains to static physical control over space (or time), but rather to the ability to control the flow of ideas, mobile 'subjects', and so on – a theme to which we will return in Chapter 4.[40] Contrary to the solid concepts upon which people could hinge an existential sense of worth, the liquid concepts now invoked are inherently volatile: liquids travel easily, dissolve and mix one another and generally behave in less predictable ways than do solids.

This lessening of predictability corresponds with a notion of time (and its relationship to space) that breaks with that which character-ised classical modernity.

One of the reasons that Bauman's imagery works so well is pre-cisely that it captures the changes that have occurred to concep-tions of how past, present and future hang together and hence the objectification of any particular period. Liquids, after all, 'never fix space nor bind time' as Bauman points out.[41] Taken together, we can see how Heller's understanding of an absolute present tense, Laïdi's crisis of meaning and Bauman's concept of liquidity all constitute attempts to capture essential (insofar as that is possible) features of our time: they capture parts of the intellectual scaffolding of the con-temporary age. In so doing, these authors together point to the idea that in the present postmodern age, rationalising the present is more complicated. Attempts to marginalise the present, to squeeze it into insignificance between an indisputable past (indisputable because it brought us here) and a knowable, utopian, future appear naive and hollow. This in turn makes 'holding on' to the present or rationalis-ing it difficult. This, I venture to say, makes the (postmodern) present a *radical* present. Among the consequences of living in absolute pre-sent tense is that although we may still entertain hopes about where we want to go, our belief in the inescapability of progress towards those goals, in the attainability of a greater good, has been irrefuta-bly shattered. It is increasingly difficult to connect the present to a vision of a compelling future. The present then becomes nothing and everything at once. In other words, it is *endless*.

In this present, we rely ever more on narratives or stories that help us make sense of the world around us. Castells calls this quest for meaning a 'culture of real virtuality', a culture 'that transcends and includes the diversity of historically transmitted systems of represen-tation: the culture of real virtuality where make-believe is belief in the making'.[42] Recall the idea invoked at the outset of this chapter that 'policing wars' are by their very logic endless or perpetual wars. The notion of war as a policing exercise – to which there is no definitive end – sits easily with a collective consciousness in which the past, present and future no longer are conjoined in a linear sequence. Just as present-day action is increasingly self-referential and we are living in an absolute present tense or 'radical present', war too has become more self-referential. The waning of the teleological worldview and with it the positing of absolute future goods has meant that war no longer takes place in an 'insignificant' present as it did in the modern period: the present is no longer marginalised in our imagination but rather amplified. In this 'era of instantaneity' war is rationalised on its own terms. The metaphorical understanding of war as policing has caught on through its necessary focus on the present in and of itself, as an end in itself. The following section shows how the consciousness that arises from the idea of a present no longer understood with reference to the past and future is manifest in the contemporary imagination of war.

## War in an endless present

The conceptual category of time and temporality is used in this chapter to open up for the possibility that there is something more fundamental going on than simply an intermingling of war and policing activity or practices, as suggested in much of the literature.[43] In order to understand why certain ideas – such as the imagination of war metaphorically as policing – catch on when they do, we need to consider the models by which an era understands itself. The sections to follow will discuss aspects of war that relate to, or have a bearing on, the way in which the 'present' appears in the contemporary discourses on war: specifically, how those rationalising the activity of war, notably through the devising of military strategies and doctrines, cope with the end of telos and living in a radical present. First, I consider the seeming lack of decisiveness in contemporary war; second, the seeming preoccupation with *warfare* over war is discussed; and third, I examine the liberal world's understanding of its enemies in present-day confrontations and conflicts. These features are prominent in the wars in Afghanistan and Iraq, and they are of particular significance to the question of how the logics of war and policing are becoming increasingly indistinct.

### The end of decisiveness in war

In the past, wars have more often than not functioned as key arbiters in international affairs. War determined 'rightful' heirs to thrones, settled disputes between states over the control of territory, economic competition and so on. War was the vehicle of popular uprising against authority (the French Revolution), a tool for the spread

of ideas (the Revolutionary Wars of the Napoleonic age); war entailed conquest and domination on one extreme, and the end of tyranny and national liberation on the other.[44] The First World War brought an end to the age of empire and redrew Europe's political map, while the Second World War halted Hitler's onslaught and established the US and the USSR as the key power centres in the world.

It no longer seems that war functions as an 'arbiter of affairs', however. Indeed, this is what British General Rupert Smith asserts when he states that 'war as conventionally known' no longer exists. War, Smith tells us, is no longer 'a massive deciding event in international affairs', nor can it be expected to be.[45] Even a cursory glance at Iraq and Afghanistan would appear to confirm Smith's assertion. In Iraq, Saddam Hussein's regime was toppled after twenty days while the Taliban government in Afghanistan had retreated from all major Afghan towns less than five weeks after the US-led invasion – yet war continued (largely unabated) in both these locations. The ostensibly decisive acts of removing both Saddam Hussein's and the Taliban regimes have by no means made those wars deciding events. A few weeks into their respective campaigns American and British officials made statements to the effect that that wars were more or less over: George W. Bush's declaration of 'an end to major combat operations' in Iraq is perhaps the most glaring example.[46] The onus soon shifted from the pursuit of war as a deciding event – which one would know was over because it had brought decisive change – to the pursuit of a viable 'exit strategy', a kind of non-ending, or at least not a decisive one.[47]

How then should the lack of decisiveness in contemporary wars be explained? The idea that war can produce decisive outcomes is bound up in the first place with the notion of war as a tool usable to realise a known and attainable goal – an ambition that is then either satisfied or thwarted through war. Either way, war's capacity to produce a decisive outcome is *actualised* in the conceptualisation of war as a tool or instrument for a known aim. This is essentially the understanding of war brought to us by Clausewitz, who famously wrote that 'war is not merely an act of policy but a true political *instrument*, a continuation of political intercourse, carried on with other means'.[48] The subtlety lies in Clausewitz's understanding of the proper relationship between politics and military strategy – that is, in the distinction between *Zweck* and *Ziel*. *Zweck* generally means 'purpose', but is used in Clausewitz's *On War* to refer to the *political objective* for which the war is fought. *Ziel*, on the other hand, generally means 'aim', but in Clausewitz's writings refers specifically to what the military commander is trying to achieve.[49] Clausewitz's instruction was for *Zweck* to always dominate *Ziel*.[50] In fact, the latter only even makes sense and acquires meaning if it is subordinate to the former. That is, military or strategic gain is completely void of consequence or value unless it fits into and is derived from the fundamental political aims in war.[51] If *Zweck* and *Ziel* are conflated, or if leaders fail to bring out the difference between them, the risk is overwhelming that any true sense of direction in war is lost. Of course, this distinction assumes that there is in fact a clear political objective in the first place – or else there would be nothing to confuse.

The lack of a clear political objective is one of the things Rupert Smith laments most in his indictment of contemporary Western war. At the time of the Kosovo campaign, when Smith served as Deputy Supreme Allied Commander Europe (DSACEUR) of the NATO forces, he writes:

> at no point before or during the bombing campaign was there a clear expression of a long-term political purpose. Was this action to create an independent Kosovo? Or was it to cause Milosevic to be deposed, to change the regime in Belgrade to one that could govern Kosovo to the UN's satisfaction?

In precisely this way, the lack of clear political purpose beleaguered narratives of the wars in Afghanistan and Iraq. Attacking the Taliban regime over its harbouring of Osama bin Laden and other senior al-Q'aeda members posited as political purpose the capture or killing of bin Laden and bringing down the Taliban regime. Moving the goalposts from regime change to 'bringing democracy to Afghanistan' and making Afghanistan inhospitable to al-Q'aeda diminished the potential for decisiveness in that war. The Iraq war took discussions over political objective to a level that was nothing short of absurd: the lack of an understandable *Zweck* was constitutive of the war from the outset as the purported existence of weapons of mass destruction, invasion on 'humanitarian' grounds and general opposition to 'terrorism' merged into an incomprehensible political tangle prior to the invasion, obliterating any proper discussion of whether the

*Zweck* posited was indeed a plausible one.[52] When President Bush declared the 'end of major combat operations' (posing in front of a sign saying 'mission accomplished', although he did not actually use those words) this may of course be seen as the realisation of an original *Zweck* – the removal of Saddam Hussein from office and regime change in Iraq. But if so, it simultaneously signalled how an ostensible original *Zweck* had been reduced to a temporary *Ziel*, for the ousting of Saddam meant little in terms of the goals that the US-led coalition was now ostensibly there to fulfil – loftily phrased in terms of 'bringing democracy to Iraq'.

The supreme confusion of *Zweck* and *Ziel* is perhaps even better illustrated by the substantial debate that took place about a 'lack of planning' for the 'post-conflict phase' in Iraq. Both the American and British political leadership was heavily criticised not only by analysts but by their respective military institutions for failing to grasp ahead of time the chaos that ensued as competing forces rushed to fill the power vacuum created post-Saddam, the widespread looting and general havoc wrecked upon ordinary Iraqis. Yet casting the debate in those terms – a lack of *planning* for a 'post-conflict phase' – the underlying problem was effectively obscured. What the aftermath of Saddam's fall from power illustrated was rather the lack of a plausible *Zweck* in the first place to which *Ziel* could be subordinated. This was of course rather helpful for the political leadership: blaming the ensuing descent into chaos in Iraq on bureaucratic infighting and other practical failings seems a lot less threatening and humiliating than admitting to the underlying problem of no-one being entirely sure what the ultimate political purpose of the war was. In that context, 'planning' effectively for it became chimerical.

The attempt by the US Central Command (CENTCOM) to re-brand the global war on terror 'The Long War' (a formulation that also made it into the *Quadrennial Defense Review* of 2006) is illustrative in its overt acceptance of the interminability of the struggle that the US had involved itself in.[53] In the same way, the statement by then US Secretary of Defense Donald Rumsfeld that 'the Iraq war will be won when Americans feel secure again' is worth highlighting for the mockery it makes of a realistic *Zweck*.[54] Rumsfeld's statement testifies to the ambivalence and anxiety inherent in a worldview that does not conceive of the present as a bridge to the future (something that can be treated instrumentally) but that demands instead that the present be legitimated on its own terms. The lack of decisiveness in contemporary wars can thus be explained in part by the insecurity over ultimate ends, from which the hesitancy over *Zweck* is derived. In other words, in a radical present, the conflation of *Zweck* and *Ziel* is perhaps only to be expected. Resigned to non-decisive war, policymakers and military leaders alike speak increasingly of 'progress' in war – a relational concept that refuses to be definitive or decisive. However, the lack of decisiveness in war would also appear to be related to the way in which wars are waged. True to their sense of living in an absolute present tense, Western leaders seem increasingly preoccupied with *warfare*, rather than the aim or purpose of war.

## A preoccupation with warfare over war

As Charles Taylor has pointed out, the abandonment of teleological perspectives – of absolute ends – raised the prospect that 'everything would become a matter of means'.[55] The focus on warfare rather than war can be understood precisely in this way: as a preoccupation with the 'how' of war over the 'why' or 'what for'. In the first instance, consider the attempt to make war more 'humanitarian', more 'civilianised' or less cruel – a proclaimed aim of contemporary Western war.[56] In the attempt to narrate war as an instrument in the creation of order, Western war is not simply waged in the interest of liberal values but is intended to *incarnate* those values. Much has thus been made of the mixing of humanitarian and military efforts, whereby militaries are expected to carry out tasks such as the protection of refugees, the delivery of aid and so on.[57] In short, war is construed as being concerned with 'protection' and rationalised as essentially productive of a new order – a manifestation of the implicit expectation that the *means* of war will somehow become the *essence* of war. Again, this accords well with the idea of the present era as one of 'instantaneity' in Bauman's terms – one in which we live in an absolute present tense, decoupled from the past and future.

In this era of instantaneity, we see a shift in emphasis from the 'strategic' to the 'tactical', the immediate. Military strategists have placed great onus on this shift: in Rupert Smith's words: 'most fights do not go to the strategic level: war amongst the people is mostly a tactical event, with occasional forays into the theatre level'.[58] The fact that Smith can insist that war is tactical reinforces the conclusion that *Zweck* and *Ziel* are being confused – not, of course, in the sense that people have lost the ability to recognise the conceptual distinction but because somehow the distinction seems to be irrelevant in practice. To emphasise this point further: it is not merely that the tactical is strategic; the tactical is *political*. Whereas critical analysts of war recognise precisely the futility of distinguishing between 'political', 'strategic' and 'tactical' 'levels' of war, what is striking about contemporary debates is that this insight is commonplace also among those who write in service of the military profession. The lament that contemporary Western warfare places too many exigencies on individual soldiers (as 'humanitarians', 'politicians', 'diplomats' and so on) is typical; and on the other hand commentators close to military circles infer that any isolation of 'exclusively military tasks' is illusory.[59]

Yet another indication of the shift in focus from the objectives of war to the means of war inheres in the conflation of political aims with the actual use of force. Rather than winning decisive battles at the strategic level, Western militaries claim to 'provide the security conditions' that will allow *non-military* efforts to be made. This (re)conceptualisation of the 'objective' of war as the maintenance of particular 'conditions' is a radical one: it posits as *the point of war the effective continuation of war itself.*[60] In essence, contemporary war is less about winning than about *transforming.* This is what has led some people to describe current war efforts as 'operations on the cusps', 'cusps' meaning literally 'a point of transition between different states'.[61] When transformation is the purpose, it is perhaps not surprising that we are concerned more with the means than the ends of war; after all, the force employed is intended not simply to usher in change (navigate the cusp) but to actually *enact* that change. Warfare has then become the essence of war. So too does the priority given to 'sustaining the mission' (for the sake of the mission) underline the point about a concern for warfare over war. Never before has 'force protection' been such an overarching concern for Western militaries; in Smith's words, 'we fight so as not to lose the force, rather than by fighting ... at any cost to achieve the aim'.[62]

The preoccupation with warfare over war is making itself known also through the focus on military activity as a species of 'risk management', a claim that has gained currency among military strategists in recent years. Authors of an emerging risk-school of strategic studies invoke primarily Ulrich Beck's theory of reflexive modernity as a metanarrative through which it is possible to interpret contemporary strategic thinking.[63] Beck's understanding of 'risk', it is claimed, not only better equips us to make sense of contemporary developments in strategic affairs; in fact it is the appropriate direction for policymakers to take. In a reflexively modern world (where modernity 'turns upon itself'), the best we can hope for is for the military is to anticipate and respond to future risks. War as a risk management exercise (or risk society war) is not concerned with ultimate aims. It is thus the antithesis of teleological worldview and there is no search for moral good in risk society. As Yee-Kuang Heng observes, risk society war is 'propelled by fear and anxiety', and thus focused on developing 'new strategies for managing risks to calm anxieties. The values system is largely negative, striving to prevent the worst rather than doing good.'[64] The concept of risk was 'operationalised' most famously by its incorporation into the US *Quadrennial Defense Review* of 2001.[65]

The understanding of strategic affairs as questions of risk management had appeal precisely because it grapples with the impossible radical/endless present. By re-interpreting the crisis of meaning that Laïdi refers to into a quest for (proactive) pre-emption of risk it would appear that some measure of purpose or directionality was restored. Yet the focus is invariably on the means and forms of war rather than its ends: on managing one's own *behaviour* so as to pre-empt future risks. What then does the preoccupation with warfare over war tell us? Could it be argued that in a radical present, where connecting past, present and future into a plausible trajectory (narrative) is so difficult, warfare has become a preoccupation in its own right? Has not only war but also warfare then become self-referential? Before turning to the consequences of the preoccupation with warfare, we will turn to a third feature of contemporary Western war that illustrates the theme of endlessness: the imagination of the opposition in narratives of US-led 'policing wars'.

### Elusive enemies; elusive victory

Contemporary wars are 'asymmetric' not simply in that they posit forces of very different strength against one another. The policing war narrative testifies to a particular image of the types of enemies confronted directly in Iraq and Afghanistan and by proxy in Somalia, Chechnya or Colombia. Opponents are not recognised in political terms but essentialised as 'terrorists' or 'criminals'.[66] In such depoliticised understanding of war, the West's imagines its own war fighting as a necessary corrective to opponents' irregular violence, variously described as 'senseless', 'meaningless' or even 'evil'.[67] When the enemy is viewed as lacking political identity or political will, there is a heightened tendency for the enemy to become less 'human' or less 'real'. In other words, the enemy becomes *elusive*.

The relatively recent practice of designating or proscribing terrorist organisations as opposed to identifying individual terrorists has contributed to such essentialisation of opponents in the contemporary Western discourse on war.[68] Then UK Home Secretary John Reid's description of the practice of proscription is instructive:

> Proscribing these groups – which are either engaged in terrorism or which glorify terrorist acts – sends a strong signal that the United Kingdom is not prepared to tolerate those who support terrorism here or anywhere in the world. ... The new, widened, criteria introduced in the Terrorism Act of 2006 ... will assist us in tackling every part of the terrorist network.[69]

The leap from identifying individuals who have committed terrorist acts to identifying groups that 'glorify terrorism' is a significant one: it reveals the elusive quality ascribed to 'enemies' under the discourse on war that emerged in the years after 9/11. The upholding of categories of people as a basis for action against individuals has notoriously led to the unlawful detention of prisoners at the US military detainment facility at Guantánamo Bay, Cuba – a practice that runs counter to individual rights under the international human rights regime created at the end of the Second World War.[70] The shift from identifying individuals who have committed criminal acts to criminalising communities can be seen in various places around the world, as evidenced in mass detentions in Chechnya or Colombia, the latter of which also saw the uncovering of mass extrajudicial killings in 2008.[71]

The idea of elusive enemies is not an original one of course, nor unique to this period. The crimes of the Nazi regime have been described as a fight against enemies 'more imagined than real' – in effect making the struggle against them 'an escape from reality'.[72] During the Nazi onslaught the imagining of the enemy as a shady creature – the enemy within society itself – served a specific function: it enabled mass indoctrination. The notion that the enemy was 'everywhere' increased fears among the German populace, creating a fire upon which the regime could continue to pour oil. In that instance, the enemies' elusiveness seemed to 'prove' the danger they ostensibly posed: portraying the enemies' existence as 'shady' and inconspicuous was extremely useful for the Nazi propagandists. Hannah Arendt has shown that this was a deliberate technique on the part of the Nazi regime, what she calls 'action as propaganda'.[73] The logic of action as propaganda is that simply by taking 'punitive' action against a group of innocent and unsuspecting people, you create the illusion that these people are in fact implicated in crime or other ill-intended action. In this way it becomes possible to blame an innocent victim for the injustices that are in fact committed *against* them. There are of course important differences in the way in which the Nazi regime conceived of its 'elusive enemies' and the way in which US-led forces have understood opponents in Afghanistan or Iraq; yet the Nazi example usefully reminds us that casting an enemy in shady, nondescript terms profoundly affects the character of war. In the case of Nazi Germany it facilitated total war, whereas in the contemporary setting it seems to do something quite different: casting the enemy as elusive serves to incorporate war and warfare into the realm of 'ordinary' politics.

In the contemporary setting, waging war against 'criminals' or 'terrorists' underlines the idea of processual war, as 'the management of insecurity' in risk terminology. This is a double bind, for in a war against apolitical ('criminal/terrorist') and elusive opponents you can neither win nor concede defeat. To concede defeat would entail resignation to criminality/terrorism, and here the elusiveness of the perceived enemy plays an important role. We saw in Chapter 1 various permutations of the theme of depoliticising non-Western parties to conflict, in policy-adjacent literature and in actual policy discourses. The process of depoliticising opponents in war (and by extension, depoliticising war itself) is intrinsically linked to the ascribing of elusiveness to the enemy: an enemy who is 'senseless' or 'irrational' cannot be but elusive. Judith Butler in *Precarious Life: The Powers of Mourning and Violence* (2004) highlights the fear of explanation at work:

> we tend to dismiss any effort at explanation, as if to explain these events would accord them rationality, as if to explain these events would involve us in a sympathetic relationship with the oppressor, as if to understand there events would involve building a justificatory framework for them.[74]

The fear of explanation as exoneration is endemic to the narrative of policing wars: if the resistance to 'order-creating war' is conceived as legitimate political resistance the narrative becomes impossible to sustain. The understanding of war as an instrument in the creation and maintenance of order makes war logically perpetual: policing, by its very nature, occurs continuously in society, and as such it is not an aberration or interruption of the normal state of affairs but, instead, precisely an indication of normality. Semiotician Umberto Eco makes precisely this point. Eco differentiates between past 'paleo-owars' (where the contenders' identity was never in doubt, thus enabling the neutrality of others) and current 'neo-wars', where the identity of the enemy is uncertain, and there is no geographical frontline.[75] In the present context, Eco writes, we may still have smaller paleowars, but these paleowars 'settle nothing except on the level of the psychological satisfaction of the temporary winner'; resulting in 'a form of permanent neowar with lots of peripheral paleowars forever breaking out and forever being ended temporarily'.[76] The important wars – the real ones – are all neo-wars, and as such they have 'no victors and no vanquished'.[77]

In the first part of the chapter it was argued that radical presentism is central to the current collective consciousness. The decline of teleological thinking and linear historicity produced a crisis of meaning such that the 'absolute present tense' is fundamental to the postmodern intellectual scaffolding. Focusing on the means of war represents an attempt to negotiate the uncertainty-inspiring radical present; conversely, this temporality sustains the imagery of perpetual policing wars, waged not against distinct and finite entities but as 'categories' of people or behaviour ('criminals'/'terrorists') universally shunned. US General Stanley A. McChrystal's statement on the war in Afghanistan epitomises the perpetuity logic: 'you can kill Taliban forever', he proclaimed, 'because they are not a finite number'.[78] In the policing war logic, new enemies are added for every one taken out, and war appears perpetual.

## The meaning of perpetual war

When Donald Rumsfeld proclaimed that the war in Iraq would not be over 'until Americans felt safe again' he can be seen to allude not only to the centrality of that war to the American political scene but to the difficulty in imagining a conclusive end to America's military enterprise in Afghanistan or Iraq.[79] Goals and objectives have been formulated and re-formulated on a continuous basis in relation to both wars, by both Bush and Blair subsequent administrations. This chapter has been about the ability of the postmodern world to believe in the purported 'goals' of respective intervention – goals that proved ever-shifting. It is here that we find the waning of teleological thinking to be the most significant: without the framework 'within which everything could be understood or explained', belief in stipulated political goals has become significantly more difficult to sustain. The implications of policing wars being perpetual or endless wars are significant – politically and ethically as well as 'strategically' – and will be further explored in the remaining chapters. Suffice at this stage to draw out two points that follow most clearly from a reading of contemporary Western war from the perspective of time and temporality.

### The demise of instrumental war

The sense of living in an absolute present tense affects the potential for an instrumental use of military force, in the way it has conventionally been understood. The view of the Western way of war as quintessentially instrumental is widely held, and generally traced back to Clausewitz. Yet the focus on warfare over war and the definition of the West's own warfare as a policing exercise directed against criminality/terrorism/disorder may be seen to imply that war is more expressive than instrumental. Proponents of policing wars rationalise these wars as wars that 'express liberal values'. In this vein, Laurence Freedman calls ours an age of liberal wars, by which he means primarily that a vital source of legitimacy for the use of military force is that it is being used 'in pursuit of essentially liberal values'.[80] More specifically, Freedman defines 'liberal wars' as wars 'conducted in pursuit of a humanitarian agenda, and which are likely to lead to a pressure for domestic political reform and reconstruction'.[81] This demands that war in fact *expresses* those values: that warfare is conducted in a manner that is in fact 'liberal'. Were it that liberal states were successful in this, it might lead to the conclusion of policing wars being both instrumental and expressive: instrumental in the sense that they are conceived as tools in the service of a particular end (liberal democracy in other states), and expressive in the sense that they express those very values they are seeking to install. In fact the opposite seems true: current illiberal practices in war – notably the use of torture and extraordinary rendition – appear intended to send a message rather than being a means to achieve an end.[82] An alternative interpretation of the dissonance between contemporary liberal and illiberal war might be that what is being 'expressed' is in fact the absence of a message. The feat of living in an endless present, it has been argued in this chapter, can be seen to compel leading states to recast war as (risk) 'management', as a process to which there is no apparent end. Seen in this light, what is expressed in contemporary policing wars is neither distinctly liberal nor illiberal but rather a form of technocratic disinterestedness – signalling an anonymous, technical-managerial approach to war.

## A normalisation of war

A second implication of the discussion of war in an endless present has to do with the way in which normality is accorded with exceptionality in contemporary international politics. Seeing war as a process rather than as a definitive and decisive act normalises war in the sense that war-fighting becomes part of undertakings that are far broader and more generic than war itself. The currency of terms such as 'stabilisation', 'state-building', 'counterinsurgency' and so on is indicative of the normalisation of war in a collective consciousness that ascribes supreme importance to the present. 'Stabilisation operations', 'state-building' and so on are practices that are composed – crucially – of military and non-military components, more often than not with an emphasis on the non-military ones. The invoking of 'social work' and 'basic social and political problems' in the US Army/Marine Corps Counterinsurgency doctrine FM 3–24 amply illustrates the extent to which the war effort has become integrated with efforts towards social order more broadly; so too does the claim by one commentator that the appropriate goal of COIN operations is the creation of 'a better normality'.[83] When normalised, war too becomes 'liquid' as per Bauman's phrase: it no longer stands as a means to an end but as a normalised process, an exercise in management, to which there is no end. Ironically, the fact that counterinsurgency campaigns are often seen as 'too costly, controversial, painful or inconclusive' is not taken as essentially damaging: there seems to be a growing acceptance that 'counterinsurgency is all of these things, and always will be'.[84] COIN, in other words, appears to quite literally to be trapped in an 'endless present'.

Moreover, defining enemies in universal(-ising) terms ('terrorists', 'criminals') allows for the process of war to become anonymised. War is then more easily integrated into or appropriated by a large apparatus involving civilian agencies, non-governmental organisations, private military and security companies and so on – a host of actors that are not, in fact, politically mandated in any sense comparable to states. Non-state actors are easily co-opted into the 'apolitical' quest that is not intended to break an enemy or decisively win a war but to create faith in a particular system of order and governance. With this recasting of war as a continuous or endless process, the act of outsourcing it to actors other than the military, such as private security companies, is hardly surprising. In this context, wars have become perpetual or endless for the simple reason that it is too difficult to imagine a conclusive end to them. The point about waging war against abstract/universal, as opposed to real and known, enemies is central here. It posits a double bind that is intrinsic to 'policing wars': you cannot fight and win against an abstract enemy, nor is it possible to concede defeat.

# 3
# Policing the Globe

## Introduction: space/spatiality and understandings of war

Understandings of war – its shape, form, character and content – are conditioned by conceptualisations and narratives of social and political space. As such, the history of writing on war is also a history of spatiality, expressed through a particular circumstance and practice: that of war. Space and spatiality, in other words, contributes significantly to the intellectual scaffolding upon which understandings, narratives and discourses of war rests. In the attempt to explain how and why the discourse of war metaphorically 'as' policing has emerged, this chapter accounts for the shift from an early modern spatial imagination and the conception of politics and war promoted by it, to contemporary understandings of space/spatiality, and its bearing on the discourse of war as policing, metaphorically understood.

Space can be understood both in material and ideational terms. Indeed, as globalisation theorist Jan Aart Scholte points out, space as a category eschews easy demarcations between material and ideational claims: space is both an *explanandum* (something to be explained) and an *explanans* (something that – partly – explains).[1] Social sciences in the last two decades have been greatly influenced by analyses of the condition of globality – of the phenomenon of globalisation, in short. So too has the analysis and theorisation of war been preoccupied with the realm of the global and new ways of understanding space/spatiality. As Paul Hirst suggests, war is 'action in a resistant medium', where 'a good deal of that resistance is associated with the qualitative spatial properties of specific forms of war'.[2] For Scholte, 'no description

57

of social circumstance is complete without a spatial component, [and] no social explanation is complete without a geographical dimension (...) A reconfiguration of social geography is intimately interlinked with shifts in patterns of knowledge, production, governance identity, and social ecology.'[3] Reading war from the perspective of spatiality, then, is productive for it shows how understandings of social phenomenon (including war), and the conception of politics therein, are premised on and conditioned by particular understandings of space/spatiality. 'Politics' in and of war refers here simply to accounts of confrontation, antagonism or conflict in political terms as being intrinsic to the phenomenon of war, derived from Clausewitz' phenomenological understanding of war as 'an act of force to compel the enemy to do our will'. This understanding is rivalled by the policing war narrative, where 'war' is conceived as an ordering practice in response to the 'disorder' of others' violence.[4]

In order to unpack a second facet of the intellectual scaffolding upon which the policing war narrative rests, I turn first to the materialities and epistemologies of war produced by early modern conceptualisations of space. This section establishes the potency of space–politics–war as a complex whole in the modern imagination, as well as its lingering impact as an ideal type centred on the state as the site of politics. Second, I turn to contemporary understandings of space/spatiality and the relationship between postmodern understandings of space/spatiality and the policing war narrative. The turn to the category of space in this chapter thus adds to the story of *why*, more profoundly, the depoliticisation of war under the policing logic proved so resonant in the early twenty-first century. What understandings of political space do we countenance in order that the trope of 'policing' has become so widespread in liberal discourses of war?

## Early modern spatialities

In his *An Anatomy of the World – the Frailty and Decay of the Whole World* (1611) poet John Donne depicted the crumbling of feudal loyalties in Europe:

> 'Tis all in peaeces, all cohaerance gone;
> All just supply, and all Relation:
> Prince, Subject, Father, Sonne, are things forgot,

For every man alone thinks he hath got
To be a Phoenix, and that there can bee
None of that kinde, of which he is, but hee.

Donne's poem is invoked by Stephen Toulmin in his careful dissec-
tion of the origins and trajectory of the early modern period to show
how the dismantling of social ties of fealty/master–subject relations
gave rise to alarm about an impending end to social cohesion. The
emergence of 'masterless men', unfettered by the 'vertical claims of
reciprocal obligation that had been constitutive of traditional society', seemed a release of grave consequence – 'tis all in peaeces' [all is
broken].[5] Until this juncture, vertical feudal ties had coexisted with
the horizontal ties of Church decision-making and spatial structure
of power. The breakdown of feudal structures and the diminishing of
the clergy's power ushered in a re-ordering of European societies, in
turn accelerated by the spread of literacy and social awareness. This
tilted the imagination of political space away from the verticality of
feudalism and horizontality of clerical power ties towards the spatiality of the sovereign state, familiarly envisaged as a container with
knowable spatial (territorial) boundaries.[6]

Far from a simple question of practical alignment, the shift towards
the state as the most politically salient trope of the modern consciousness concerned the way in which people relate to one another.
Put differently, the conceptualisation of political space was then, and
is now, a productive way of investigating the way in which people
make sense of their relationship to one another – a fundamental part
of social and political interaction. Seeing a complex whole is the
very essence of Toulmin's account: 'cosmos' is the traditional Greek
word for the Order of Nature, to which people are born and which
is evidenced in the cycle of seasons, tides and so on – events that do
not occur by chance but according to a pre-given order; and 'polis',
on the other hand, equates to the Order of Society – the elements
created under human control, including such collective enterprises
as the administration of cities, the organisation of irrigation systems
and so on: systems designed with an overall coherence that qualifies
them as a 'political' units.[7] Bringing 'cosmos' and 'polis' together
captures the fact that from the emergence of large-scale human society, people have wondered about the links between *cosmos* and *polis*,
between what Nature has prearranged and what Humans themselves

determine and create. What occurred with the shift to modernity was nothing less than a crisis of cosmopolis: after 1610, Toulmin tells us, 'Europe's loss of all social, political, and spiritual cohesion had moved beyond all remedy'.[8]

The secularisation of authority did not just enable the creation of the modern state, but simultaneously intensified the 'burden of justification' of political rule, as Ian Loader and Neil Walker point out.[9] Hobbes' view of legitimate political rule as the collective escape of citizens from a state of nature in constant war of 'all against all', through the creation of a social contract and embodied in the Leviathan, was a response precisely to this call for justification of political rule (made urgent through the English Civil War). As innovator of the very concept of the modern state, Hobbes' findings were doubly important with respect to the spatiality of the modern political imagination. Beyond the potency of his argument about the unifying capacity of the state, Hobbes' notion of the state as 'a purely abstract entity – *a persona ficta* – separate from both the sovereign, who may nevertheless bear much of the authority of the state, and from the ruled' is significant.[10] This abstractness of the Hobbesian Leviathan is a topic that has preoccupied among others Quentin Skinner, who sees this as the 'doubly abstract' or 'doubly impersonal' character of the modern state.[11] Hence, the understanding brought by Hobbes as regards the conceptualisation of space adds an abstract dimension (the 'persona' of the state) to the otherwise concrete dimensions of the modern, unified and territorial state.

From this abstracted unity of the state and the modern discourse on political organisation and ruling/rule, another attribute of modern spatiality emerges: the necessary, indeed compulsory, territoriality of modern politics. This is what Max Weber pointed to in his sociology of the modern state, which he described as 'a compulsory organisation with a territorial basis'.[12] The modern state thus relied expressly on the visual image of geographical territory, where borders drawn on maps mark the boundaries of the 'state' (as administrator/ruler with claim to jurisdiction) and its capacity to effect its will through political acts. The boundedness of the state – the container image – is thus its key spatial characteristic: its *raison d'être* and legitimacy rests on the clear physical demarcation of its being. Conceptualisations of space always involve the consideration of politics – 'the processes of acquiring, distributing and exercising social power' – and, in the early modern spatial imagination, political power was conceived of as being inherently territorial.[13]

Epistemological prioritisation of knowable, material 'political' space also underpinned specific practices in the early modern period: Weber's administrative order would not be possible without the territorial foundation of the state; and the construction of citizenship (obtained by the locality of one's birth, rather than religious identity or feudal affiliation) similarly underlined the automaticity and compulsory nature of early modern spatiality. Importantly, the territorially bound state translated directly into Weber's understanding of the use of force.[14] The Weberian understanding of state/space was naturalised in the modern era, so much so that territoriality acquired a 'taken-for-grantedness' in social theory.[15] For Michael Mann, this means that the state possessed *autonomous power*, a quality that sets it apart from other power groupings of 'civil society', the most important source of this autonomy being its centralised and territorial nature.[16] The state, Mann tells us, 'is, indeed, a *place*'.[17]

For Toulmin, the emergence of the modern state was sustained, both materially and epistemologically, by the modern desire for exactitude – at once a philosophical and an aesthetic preference, manifest in the assertion of scientificity and the absence of scepticism.[18] In other words, there was a neat match between the institution of the modern state, the 'compulsory organisation with a territorial basis', and the intellectual scaffolding of the seventeenth century onwards. One reinforced the other: the state fitted with the modern preoccupation with science, exactitude, rationality and so on; and that structure of ideas in turn facilitated the establishment of the modern state. The term used by political geographer John Agnew in this instance is apt: to Agnew the naturalisation of state space in the modern era is such that we can conceive of a 'geographical unconscious'.[19] Brian Turner's understanding similarly seizes on the constitutive impact of spatiality on human consciousness: modernity, Turner tells us, 'was about conquest, the imperial regulation of land, the discipline of the soul, and the creation of truth'.[20] The potency of early modern space/spatiality is particularly clear as we consider its constitutive impact on the imagination and rationalisation of war – paving the way for an intimate connection between war, space and politics in the modern imagination.

## Space, politics and war in the modern imagination

By establishing a relationship between the consolidation of the state as a political, legal and moral entity, and the phenomenon of war, Charles Tilly addresses both the materiality and epistemology of modern spatiality.[21] 'Recognition of the *centrality* of force opens the way to an understanding of the growth and change of governmental forms,' Tilly tells us; thus, 'war making, extraction and capital accumulation interacted to shape European state making'.[22] The link between the state as physical/juridical/administrative body (its material being) and its capacity/predisposition for war is thus established – a link that confirms the general epistemological importance of space/spatiality for understanding war, including the post 9–11 'policing wars'. The adage that 'war made the state, and the state made war' crudely abbreviates the more complex account Tilly gives of how the activities of the modern state reinforce and are reinforced by distinct forms of organisation – all related to consolidation, centralisation and territorialisation.[23]

The philosophical and aesthetic preference for order and predictability (centred on territorial understandings of politics) in turn caused, reflected, and was reflected in, the modern state's relationship with war. The geometric precision of the territorial state was matched by similar desire for exactitude in warfare: via recourse to works of art as well as literature in the late seventeenth and early eighteenth century, cultural historian John Lynn vividly illustrates the Enlightenment era's penchant for *linear warfare*.[24] Linearity in war, Lynn is careful to point out, has two meanings: 'on the one hand it denotes lines, as the neat formation of troops ...; on the other it refers to predictability, as in a linear equation. Both meanings apply to warfare in the age of the Enlightenment.'[25] In other words, the affinities between the state and the modern desire for exactitude are reflected also in the twin connotations of linearity: the desire for regularity, predictability and rationality was both more profound and more widely shared than to be confined to any discussion of war alone.

Geometrical preoccupation, both aesthetic and philosophical, is recognisable in various aspects of war and warfare in the early modern period. The linearity of formation in the battlefield is evocative of the centralising tendencies of modern modes of organisation.

The presumption and desiring of predictability chimes with the concreteness of clearly demarcated physical space. This is early modern aesthetics – that which is 'clear, easily grasped' – what Lynn calls a 'military enlightenment', whereby 'rational and scientific forms' imposed themselves on military operations and tactics.[26] Again, it is form that is of greatest interest to us here, signifying the spatial dimension of modern warfare. The French introduction of uniforms in the seventeenth century also satisfied both an aesthetic demand and the desire for order, exactness and strict physical formation.[27] The use of fortifications emerged as an essential feature of *Ancien régime* warfare, along with sieges and other geometrically informed battle tactics.[28]

Both siege warfare and fortifications constitute quintessential examples of geometrical aesthetics and the modern preference for a definitive spatial imagination. In fact, the distinction between siege and battle can be said to be illusory as it obscures their conceptual similarity: the favouring of scientificness and predictability along with the dismissal of chaos and openness.[29] We find similar ambition to control battle by confining it to a limited physical space in the use of fortifications – they too could be made into 'ideal engineered battlefields'. The 'military enlightenment' had no shortage of written sources from its own time: Antoine-Henry Jomini (1779–1869) was central in emphasising geometrical thinking; so too Maurice de Saxe (in *Rêveries,* 1757) expresses a 'desire for rationalized, intellectualised war ... [that was] orderly and predictable'.[30] In this spatially determinate version of war, the ideal of the decisive battle reigned. Napoleon's Battle at Austerlitz in 1805 was a spectacular example of high-precision encounter where spatial dimensions were carefully calculated.[31] The modern history of space was thus conjoined with particular understandings of war: sieges and fortifications mirror the territoriality of the state on the battlefield and linearity embodied the philosophical preference for order.

Importantly, the desire for linearity, predictability, exactitude and scientific knowability furthered an adjacent imagination of politics along clear, physical spatial lines. In the modern imagination, war entailed political confrontation; and the definitive spatiality of politics/war/political war prompted a similarly concrete, discrete and linear understanding of political antagonism, of competition and political strife. Space–politics–war emerged as a complex whole and a central trope of the modern imagination, centred on the territorial nation-state. This spatiality of modern war thus contained within it an account of power struggle and political antagonism, whereby political conflict was understood in terms of control of the state; and political resistance entailed resistance of the state. This view has had a profound impact on the conceptual categories of mainstream understandings of war. To illustrate: leading quantitative research programmes depict war as being *necessarily* tied to the state, categorising conflicts as being tied to the state in one of two ways, either as conflicts over the control of territory (separatist) or over the control of government.[32] In other words, if it doesn't centre on the state, it isn't a conflict proper.

Of course, the early modern period was also the age of empire, of colonial conquest through military expansion on the part of the European imperial powers from the fifteenth century onwards. Imperial expansion can be seen to indicate a second incarnation of early modern spatiality: first, the territorial nation-state, and second, the global extension of the imperial, but nonetheless territorial state's power. Notions of frontiers and borderlands are central to the spatial imagery of the early modern period and stand out as the ostentatious extension of the social and political spatiality of the individual nation state. The spatial imagery of classical empire is thus still very much an expression of the materiality/physicality of early modern spatiality of the state: a projection of fixed, territorial spatiality, rather than in contrast to or in conflict with it. The age of (classical) empire, in other words, saw the modern state extend to project its power on the global level precisely through its physicality: the exercise of modern, physical, material, territorial power of one state over another. In this way, while 'empire' as trope and metaphorical imagery recurs in contemporary debates on war, the spatialities invoked are fundamentally different from the firmly territorial spatiality of early modern imperial conquest.

## Contemporary spatialities: war and the end of territorialism

'I suppose the danger we will have to fight back in the coming century won't be totalitarian coercion, the main preoccupation of the century that just ended, but the falling apart of "totalities" capable of securing the autonomy of human societies.'[33] Zygmunt Bauman's words captured an essential sensibility of the post-Cold War period: the notion that the state no longer possessed the same capacity, role or function as accorded to it in the early modern political imagination. From Susan Strange's early statement of the 'retreat of the state' under the influence (primarily) of global capital, a range of authors depicted a world that had moved 'beyond sovereignty', that was 'post-Westphalian', dominated by 'non-state', 'sub-state' or 'transnational' powers and dynamics.[34] It is widely asserted, then, that the most significant feature of postmodern spatiality is the process of globalisation constituting a challenge to the state's capacity and the emergence of rivalling social, political and ethical forms of association; or the way national structures combine with new spatial (and temporal frames).[35] Scholte's claim that we are witnessing a 'respatialization with the spread of transplanetary social connections', is significant for its assertion that notions of 'globality' and 'supraterritoriality' capture a shift in the *very nature* of social space.[36] Supraterritorial relations as 'social connections that substantially transcend territorial geography', are, then, connections with 'qualities of transworld simultaneity ... and transworld instantaneity (anywhere on the planet in no time)'.[37] To say that they take us beyond territorial*ism* is to say that they involve a novel way of understanding social and political space – one that operates beyond physical territoriality.[38] In short, Scholte's material claims about globality and supraterritoriality have both epistemological and ontological implications. What we have seen over the last decades, then, is the demise not of territory, but of territorialism; not of the state, but of statism: a 'territoriality changed by its encounter with supraterritoriality' rather than complete 'de-territorialisation'.[39]

Contemporary readings of war in different ways combine claims about a material newness of space/spatiality (such as the fact that armed groups operate 'transnationally', that their movement and connectivity is 'global', or that the Internet constitutes a 'virtual sanctuary' for individuals planning terrorist attacks) with epistemological and ontological assertions about war itself.[40] Sociologists like Ulrich Beck, Zygmunt Bauman or Manuel Castells have been influential in such debates precisely through their combining of material and non-material claims about a world that they see as less 'territorially conditioned'.[41] To illustrate, when Bauman refers to 9/11 as the 'symbolic end to the era of space', his claim is at once material and epistemological: political and social affairs take place beyond the state, Bauman claims, and they can only be known or understood through a different spatial imagination than that which passes through the sovereign state.[42] Thus the claim is made that war, peace and security are 'essentially, extraterritorial issues that evade territorial solutions'.[43] In sum, the idea of politics operating through the structures of the modern state enabled an understanding also of political strife and antagonism through violent means, in accounts of war as a political phenomenon. The modern understanding of war–space–politics as a complex whole is upset in contemporary accounts of war, as we shall see in the next sections. Turning to contemporary accounts of war, we will see how reading war from the perspective of spatiality sheds light on the relative absence of accounts of politics in current discourses on war. The discussion takes two steps: first, I consider the ways in which political spatiality can be seen to be in flux through contemporary accounts of war; and second, the seeming *insistence on the global* is discussed.

### Political spatiality in flux

The liberal interventionist plea for policing wars in an unruly world (Howard, Mueller, Kaldor) illustrates a political spatiality in flux. To begin, 'policing' on the global level is understood in metaphorical terms: there is no overarching absolute authority whose laws are policed (no Leviathan), but rather a set of dispersed practices (of which the use of military force is one) intended to contribute to an ideal of 'liberal governance'.[44] This represents a clear shift away from the sovereign state–war–politics as a complex whole in the modern spatial imagination, as well as a break with the literal meaning of 'policing' in imperial discourses. Ample illustration of the paradoxical spatial imagination inherent in the liberal intervention-thesis can be found in the ambition for military intervention to '(re)-build' states. In 2009 US Secretary of Defense Robert Gates described the wars in Iraq and Afghanistan as 'nation-building under fire', testimony to how state-building, previously conceived as a matter of post-war (re)construction, had been reconceptualised as *integral* to war itself.[45] The US Army/Marine Corps Counterinsurgency Field Manual of 2006 (FM 3–24) characterised US military ventures as fundamentally concerned with 'building functioning states' and 'out-governing' the enemy.[46]

Political imagination, as we have seen, is conditioned by spatiality. The shifting of spatial imagination from linear statism to globality and supraterritoriality has involved a fundamental upheaval of political relationships and the way in which political agency is imagined. Only in light of this can we understand the evolution of such counter-intuitive and contradictory ideas as that of military intervention (war) *(re)establishing* the social contract in *another* state, *on behalf of* another people – an idea, of course, that has very little in common with classical understandings of a social contract between state and citizen. This flux in spatial imagination is evident in what Ian Loader calls 'the contradictory state of the contemporary state'.[47] The conflation of international war with 'domestic' state-building can thus be seen as a product and reflection of postmodern fluctuating spatialities, where intervening forces (led by the US in Iraq and Afghanistan) are posited as creating 'order' in the target states through military intervention. The depoliticisation inherent in the conceptualisation of 'insurgency'/'insurrection' – tied to the criminalisation of opponents in war – is thus *coupled* with a corresponding depoliticised imagination of the intervening forces' *own* war-fighting. Rather than conceptualising their own war as war proper, involving political confrontation, intervening forces' war-fighting is posited as a technical-managerial task of 'order-creation'. In short, the metaphorical imagination of 'policing wars' is supported by a particular spatial understanding.

There is evidence of a political spatiality in flux also in the frequent attempts to marry modern and postmodern (material) spatialities and the emergence of a war-state-building complex. In this vein, various influential commentators such as Richard Haass and Anne-Marie Slaughter have drawn on Manuel Castells' notion of networks to criticise the attempt to create modern, bureaucratic states.[48] Thus, Haas and Slaughter advocate the creation of 'networked states', by which they mean a state that, besides exercising physical territorial control, should also excel at tapping the potential of global networks.[49] Similarly, in their 2008 book *Fixing Failed States*, Ashraf Ghani and Clare Lockhart identify as one of the key features of state failure that such states are 'characterised by syndromes of dysfunctionality and conflict that prevent their citizens from accessing global flows'.[50] Ghani and Lockhart go on to advocate a species of state-building premised on a *networked* understanding of the relationship between markets, state and people; and arrive at the remarkable view that states emerging out of war should be constructed as 'network states' – able to work global networks – from the start. Thus they would be 'fixed'.

The dual imperative of the externally driven state-building agenda – building modern social and political structures of the state while also building networked, fluid and flexible postmodern structures of politics – illustrates the contradictory nature of contemporary spatial imagination. To give an example of how this plays out in actual practice: consider the expectation that the Afghan government should exert a (historically unprecedented) state monopoly on the legitimate means of violence by building up strong state institutions, *at the same time* as it is encouraged to establish a productive relationship with potent global *non-state* actors. The global private security industry and international civil society organisations, both of which have a formidable presence in Afghanistan, thus arrived alongside the international troops operating in the country and the government is asked to find productive ways of interacting with all. Such aims reflect the confusion around political spatiality that exists within liberal decision-making circles. The ambivalence of the 'international community's' understandings of political space at the start of the twenty-first century, in other words, translates into paradoxical imperatives towards their 'local partners' in cases of military intervention, in this case the government of Afghanistan.

When counterinsurgency strategist David Kilcullen claims that 'insurgency today follows state failure, and is not directed at taking over a functioning body politic, but at dismembering or scavenging its carcass, or contesting an "ungoverned space"', his assertions at once illustrate the flux in political spatiality *and* its depoliticising effects on the understanding of war.[51] By asserting that armed groups do not necessarily aim for control over central state institutions, Kilcullen is simultaneously calling into question the politics or political nature of their fight. This illustrates the way in which modern political spatiality lingers as the conventional way of understanding the politics of war – the contestation, confrontation and antagonism that, as Clausewitz reminds us, is essential to war as a phenomenon.[52] If current accounts of war and strategic thinking have a contradictory position on the 'state of the state', this ambivalence is no less when it comes to reconciling the state with the global. The section to follow will consider a second material claim about the spatiality of contemporary war: the insistence that it takes place in a setting that is properly global.

## Insisting on the global

One of the most influential critiques of ideas and ideals liberal governance and its associated practices of military intervention to 're-build' states is found in Michael Hardt and Antonio Negri's *Empire* (2000), which since its publication has inspired what may be referred to as a biopolitical turn within security studies.[53] Hardt and Negri view 'global governance' as a euphemism for what is really a biopolitical empire, a world of 'conflict within the imperial power of empire' where 'every war is a civil war, a police action'.[54] The reference to 'policing' in these otherwise opposing bodies of thought – the liberal interventionists and their critics – is revealing.

As David Chandler rightly points out, these two ostensibly diametrically opposed schools of thought share an important commonality: they both rely on an 'essentialised connection between liberalism and global war'.[55] Where global governance advocates see a global civic movement motivated by liberal values (a term they would resist as the values are seen to be 'universal', not 'liberal'), critics equate liberalism with militarised biopolitical control, where the world as a whole is subjected to strategies for the production of life. In Hardt and Negri's terms, 'empire can only be conceived as a universal republic, a network of powers and counterpowers structured in a boundless and inclusive architecture'.[56] As Tom Lundborg and Nick Vaughan-Williams explain further, 'the tacit assumption is that the network of biopolitical relations "it" [liberal rule] entails actually "works"'.[57] Liberal biopolitical rule is seen, then, as 'a fully constituted – and "successful" – totality'.[58] If understandings of the relationship between space/spatiality–politics–war are simply cemented as a totalised and totalising biopolitical empire, then nothing is actually *explained*; it is too neat, too complete. Reliance on global spatialities (both materially and epistemologically) in the case of the war as biopolitical empire discourse entails downplaying resistance, antagonism and political conflict in war in a way that is strikingly similar to the liberal discourse on policing wars.

We find evidence of a shifting spatial imagination on strategic, tactical and operational levels alike, signifying at once new material developments and a changed ontology of space. In this vein Kilcullen refers to the contemporary condition as one where modern Cartesian systems analysis, until recently the basis for strategic thinking, has become outmoded; instead he invokes theories of complexity to advocate a 'complex systems analysis' as the basis for strategic and operational planning.[59] According to Kilcullen, viewing insurgencies as complex biological systems allows for a system of disaggregation, 'focussing on interdicting links between theatres, denying ability of regional and global actors to link and exploit actors, disrupting flows between and within jihad theatres'.[60] In a theoretical exploration of the network paradigm of strategic thinking, Antoine Bousquet draws on Manuel Castells' idea of the network as 'social morphology' to shed light on the spatiality of contemporary war.[61] In Bousquet's account, both the US and its opponents in Iraq and Afghanistan rely on net-worked forms of warfare. From 'swarming' and 'self-synchronised' American war fighting units to fluid structures of insurgent indi-viduals connected through mobile phones and web-communication, Bousquet dubs this latest turn 'chaoplexic warfare'.[62]

The insistence on globality in contemporary war is evidenced also by the fact that strategic planning increasingly refers to the global information environment as a distinct 'operational level'. From a new spatial ontology of war, military strategists like Kilcullen derive operational and tactical imperatives: in his *Twenty-eight articles: fun-damentals of company-level counterinsurgency*, for instance, Kilcullen directs each individual officer to 'keep the global audience in mind' at all times.[63] By extension, new material realities reflect an insist-ence on the global in epistemological terms (how we gain knowledge about war affects war itself). The practice of individual soldiers' blog-ging about their experiences, or the dissemination of images from war zones, constitute other material reflections of global spatiality in contemporary war.

A strong focus on globality in both material and epistemological terms is part also of what has given rise to recent theses of war as risk management.[64] Rasmussen's *Risk Society at War* (2006) invokes primarily Beck's theory of reflexive modernity as a metanarrative through which contemporary strategic thinking is interpreted under a global spatiality.[65] The 'risk society at war' thesis eschews engage-ment with political content of war, seeing the risk age as devoid of ideology and its wars as the simple pre-emption of future consequences of present-day action.[66] In a reflexively modern world where modernity is seen to turn upon itself, the risk-thesis offers scant political imperative other than the anticipation of and response to future risks. In the 'risk school' of strategic thought, in other words, war is conceived not as a political contest but as the anxious anticipation of future outcomes of present-day action – action that is global *par excellence*, for 'risks' in Beck's or Bauman's sense know no geographical boundaries.

As shown, the insistence on the global as a means of identifying spatiality in contemporary war is a theme that unifies disparate discourses: liberal governance theorists, the Hardt and Negrian biopolitics school, and theorists of war-as-risk-management. By interpreting political space/spatiality in terms of a single global whole, material claims about the global sphere are extended to ontological claims about war itself ('war *is* the collapse of politics'). The result is that many contemporary accounts of war risk verging toward spatial 'totalisation', leading either to naive optimism (the global governance view) or determinism and essentialisation (the Hardt and Negri biopolitics school).

In sum, no alternative reading of political space/spatiality has emerged in comparable force to the statism and territorialism of the (early) modern imagination. Confusion about contemporary social and political space – a political spatiality in flux – has translated into inherently contradictory practices (material realities) in war, evidenced in practices of what might be called the 'war-state-building complex' and the imperative to 'building networked states' amid occupation and war. The trope of the state as site for politics, and state–politics–war as a complex whole of the early modern imagination retains its potency to the extent that theoreticians of war suffer a collective difficulty in accounting for politics 'without sovereignty'.[67] As early modern spatialities are foregone in current debates, we see instead an overwhelming insistence on the global, as outlined in this section, which in turn unites seemingly disparate accounts of contemporary war in a collective neglect of the politics in and of war.

## Conclusion

This chapter constitutes a reading of contemporary discourses on war from the perspective of spatiality. This perspective is productive,

I have argued, for it allows us to grasp the ways in which under-standings of *politics* and *war* – two notoriously difficult and complex concepts – are conditioned by abstract notions of space and spatial-ity. This conditioning has material dimensions as conceptions of space and spatiality influence actual practices in war. Thus, we saw how the early modern period was characterised by a dominance of linear warfare, reflecting the aesthetic and philosophical preference for order. Spatial imaginations also condition the way in which we understand war – the epistemologies on which we rely. Accordingly, we saw how the understanding of politics as centred on the state was bound up with an understanding of the *politics* of war as centred on control of territory.

Attention to the social history of space/spatiality is important for it offers clues as to why there is such a dearth of accounts of politi-cal conflict in contemporary war, a key feature of the metaphorical understanding of war 'as' policing. The confusion over political spatiality – its flux – has yielded a variety of contradictory impulses: notably the practice of externally orchestrated 'state-building' amid war, and the adjacent ambition for states to be fully fledged, flexible 'network states', able to tap the potential of globality and suprater-ritoriality *not despite occupation and war, but because of it*. The disrup-tion of modern linear spatiality, both in material and epistemological terms, has affected both the imagination of war itself and the com-prehension of war as political conflict. In this chapter, accounts of contemporary war were read from the perspective of space/spatiality, revealing how departure from space–politics–war as a complex whole has led to a political spatiality in flux and an insistence on globality, which, in turn, sustains the depoliticizing narrative of war as polic-ing. Three influential accounts of contemporary war were seen to share this neglect of political antagonism as an intrinsic part of war: liberal cosmopolitans' view of resistance to their project as inciden-tal and possible to overcome (through 'policing wars' directed at the creation of order in target societies); the biopolitics view of a totalised system of control that is already in operation globally and that 'works', thus allowing scant space for resistance (that which evades control). The risk management view tackles globality but not politics; war to the risk theorists is simply the pre-emption of future consequences of present-day action – values, meaning or politics are neither here nor there.

As a result of the turn to globality in epistemological terms, we are left with an *unspatiality* of contemporary political relations, to the detriment of our understanding of the political content of war. In a sense, the metaphor of war as 'policing' has emerged precisely as a result of its unspatiality and amenability to rival interpretations. This neglect is dangerous: failing to recognise the political content of war, the essential confrontation that it constitutes, allows for the normalisation of war in contemporary political life.

# 4
# Power in Policing Wars

## Introduction

Implicit in any understanding of war is an account also of power; this
we learn from Clausewitz' understanding of war as 'an act of force
to compel the enemy to do our will'. Neither 'force' nor the act of
'compelling' can be essentially grasped without also accepting some
conception of power embedded therein. In other words, if phenomenologically we cannot separate 'war' from 'power', then reasonably
a conception of one implies a conception also of the other. In this
chapter we arrive, then, at the unpacking of a third foundational
dimension of the contemporary discourse on war as policing – the
conceptions of power upon which it rests.

It is entirely possible to discuss the means, rationalisation or function of power without committing to a metaphysical definition of
power as phenomenon. Indeed, it was one of Nietzsche's key insights
that only those matters that have no history can be defined.[1] While
this chapter in no way aspires to proper genealogical reading either in
method or scope, it nevertheless aims to offer insight into some of the
most important ways in which collective conceptions of power have
altered, and been altered by, the transition from modernity to postmodernity. Significantly, we find different notions of power underpinning
various and varied conceptualisations of politics and political life.

Before attempting to make imaginaries of power in the current era
intelligible, it is again worth casting an eye back toward the period
of classical modernity. The conceptions of power that dominated
the seventeenth and eighteenth centuries in Europe constituted the

scaffolding that sustained modern social and political structures, and so too ideals and preconceptions about modern war as a linear force. In contrast, the interventions in Iraq and Afghanistan have come to centre on the ambition for international forces to physically and metaphysically *transfer power* to local police and military. This ambition, it will be argued, is an integral part of the metaphorical understanding of war as policing, whereby the aim of the war is not to win in a conventional sense through defeating an enemy but to transfer power from one 'policing authority' to another.

## Modern conceptions of power

The history of modernity is in many ways itself a history of power, in particular as conceptions of power came to find their expression in the emergence of modern social and political institutions. Indeed, power itself became a central topic for theorists of the modern era, and one may even go so far as to claim that the act of theorising power emerged as a quintessentially modern preoccupation. The analysis of power is central to two key aspects of modern life and theorising thereof: in the first instance, thinking about power is central to theorising politics – in fact, to the very conception of politics in early modernity. Political organisation and political life as they became known in seventeenth- and eighteenth-century Europe were built on distinctly modern conceptions of power. Second, the modern understanding of power and the way it operates underwrote much of the early modern institution of the bureaucratic, industrialised state. These two themes will be considered in turn, opening up for a reading of modern war focused on the conceptualisation of power therein.

Thomas Hobbes' rendition of power in *Leviathan* established the concept as the central operating force of social and political life.[2] The strife between Parliamentarians and Royalists in England at the time of writing in the mid-1600s led Hobbes to posit anarchy as the most menacing prospect for human life. This vision was one that Hobbes took seriously enough to make it the basis of his theory of both power itself and politics, which famously posits a fictive 'state of nature' of 'Warre of All against All' as its *sine qua non*. At root, Hobbes conceived an individual's power as a simple capacity, knowable and quantifiable, defined as 'the present means to obtain some future apparent Good'.[3] Hobbes' power-as-capacity is complemented by his understanding of power [of one man] always in relation/ opposition to other men, that is, in 'the command over some of the powers of other men'. Correspondingly, he finds 'the *Value*, or WORTH of a man, is as of all other things, his Price; that is to say, so much as would be given for the use of his Power: and therefore is not absolute, but a thing dependent on the need and judgement of another'.[4] Moreover, and importantly, Hobbes assumes that some men's desire and appetite for power is unlimited; it is this assumption that completes the image of an incessant struggle for power of all against all, – in Hobbes' words, 'Man's need for power has now become a necessarily harmful thing.'[5] The relational essence of power is key in the transition from Hobbes' account of power to his account of politics: the state of nature could only be escaped, and civil life could only be harnessed, through the transferral of all men's natural powers to a sovereign authority. The establishment of a social contract is thus fundamentally a story of how power is funnelled through *consent*; it takes us from an account of power to an account of politics.

Social contractarianism is associated not only with Hobbes, of course, but equally with John Locke (*Two Treaties on Government*, 1690) and Jean-Jacques Rousseau (*The Social Contract*, 1762).[6] Yet Hobbes is the philosopher that most closely aligns his account of politics with an account of power, and in this respect his work came to occupy a pivotal position. Indeed, the key occupation of modern political theory was with the notion of a community of autonomous individuals whose deliberate consent afforded their government or sovereign the capacity and right to rule.[7] So too was the sovereign's ability to make use of his actions thought to be dependent on the consent of his subjects.[8] In this way, the modern link between power and politics was established via the idea of consent: only if people consented to being ruled could one speak of 'politics' in any sense considered proper.

Yet, the emphasis on authority as the link between power and politics did not go unchallenged in the early modern period. A point of contention was the issue of legitimacy: Hobbes for instance was less concerned with legitimacy than for example John Locke. To Hobbes, the thoughts and opinion of subjects (citizens) are of no great significance; instead it is their actual behaviour – whether they obey the rule of the Leviathan and resolve differences peacefully – that matters.[9] By contrast, the Lockean account of political power insists on the existence of *trust* (along with public reason) as an essential element of political power – an insistence that is to recur to great effect with the waning of classical modernity and the advent of more radical critique. Hobbes' contribution to the theorisation of power and politics was supremely influential above all owing to his insistence on the idea of 'power as right', firmly linking power to authority and sovereignty – in this sense his view was that power was self-legitimating.

Contractarianism stands out as a key revolution of modern political thought, tying an account of power to the notion of politics as authority. From this vantage point, we can see how a second pivotal feature of modern political life emerged: the establishment of what became understood as distinctly modern political institutions. The core agreement formed by modern social contract theorists from Hobbes to Rousseau around the existence of a political community led to the discussion of social and political institutions to govern the community in question. Most immediately we can see how the notion of power as capacity and authority, which recurs in the work of theorists of power and modernity from Hobbes to Weber, was conducive to an image of power being *channelled* through the social organisation and structure that emerged in the modern era – most importantly that of bureaucracy.

As the chief theorist of modern bureaucracy and its effects, Weber identified power with the 'the chance of a man or a number of men to realise their own will even against the resistance of others who are participating in the action'.[10] The element of resistance that Weber stresses in his understanding of power underlies also his fuller accounts of political power, which he sees as 'grounded in organized violence that is, on some people's capacity to awaken fear in others. putting at stake their survival and physical integrity'.[11] For Weber, of course, the nation-state was unrivalled in its status as the most important institutional expression of politics in the modern era. Fear or resistance on the part of the citizen/subject in no way contradicts the notion of power as authority for modern theorists. Instead it was precisely fear (especially in the work of Hobbes) that inspired citizens to consent to the authority of the state.[12]

Interesting in terms of the modern linkage established between power as capacity and authority is the issue of legitimacy, both as a corollary to power and as a potential precondition for politics. We have seen how the Hobbesian account of power as authority was less concerned with the thoughts and views of the subjects of power than with their actual behaviour (submission to the sovereign). Three centuries later, Weber gave his account of domination as being twofold: 'the first operating through the *commands* which one party gives the other (...) and the second through the *control* which the first party exercises over the circumstances in which the second acts'.[13] The first is the realm of political power, Weber tells us, and the second the realm of economic power. The two versions of power elicit different responses: in the first case power yields an assumed and unreflective obedience, derived from a person's 'existential position' (e.g. the natural authority that a parent has over a child). In the second category Weber discerns a deliberative relationship between subject and authority where subjects have some choice as to how to respond to control exercised over them. In the Weberian account, legitimacy belongs to a third category altogether, one where the moral judgement of individuals matters. For Weber, in other words, accounting for the way in which power operated in modern society did not necessarily demand an account of legitimacy.

Nowhere was this more notable than in Weber's account of inter-state relations, wherein he could see no room for a discussion of legitimacy. Rather, in inter-state relations, each state strives to define and pursue its own interests, including through war. Sovereign states in Weber's view, thus do not 'obey' or 'disobey' one another; rather, it is the actual capacity of one state to overpower or resist other states that constitutes their very relationship.[14] This realist account of power has met much resistance in the contemporary period – a resistance that is due not simply to standard critiques of realism within International Relations but also, as we shall see later on in this chapter, to the dawn of different understandings of power. One such difference as it pertains to the emergence of the discourse on 'policing wars' is the growing suspicion (contra Weber) that power and legitimacy cannot be altogether separated but, in fact, hang together. Karl Marx was of course also supremely influential in conceptualising power in the classical modern period with his complex account of how subjects may resist power exercised over them through the structures of modern industrialised society. Nevertheless, as Michael Mann points out in his *The Sources of Social Power*, the Marxist and Weberian traditions of social theory share the joint premise that 'social stratification is the overall creation and distribution of power in society'.[15] Indeed, as Mann shows, social stratification was in the modern imagination the central structure of societies owing to 'its dual collective and distributive aspects (as) the means whereby human beings achieve their goals in society'.[16]

While a growing preoccupation with class in eighteenth- and nineteenth-century Europe called into question the earlier social contract theorists' assumption about political community, this shift in focus was consistent with established conceptualisations of power. In both the social contract tradition and the Marxist understanding, power was definitely knowable (some would say quantifiable), and it was thought to operate in a predictable, linear fashion. Despite important variations between theorists from Hobbes and Rousseau to Marx and Weber, the understanding of 'power as capacity' united modern thinking on power. Modern theorists shared what Toulmin calls the three key 'pillars of rationality': certainty, systematicity and the clean slate.[17] These three pillars underpinned the philosophical programme of modernity and helped stabilise an idealised linear notion of power. This conceptualisation of power in turn informed the creation of sovereign entities in the shape of the nation-state and produced the social stratification and bureaucratic institutions that emerged in the modern industrialising state. That the same idealised notion of power would also come to influence discourses on and practices of war should be no surprise; war, after all, is as much a social and political phenomenon as any other.

### Linear power and war

Clausewitz' views on war were much influenced by his experience in the wars of the French Revolution and the later Napoleonic wars. As we saw in the previous chapter on space, linear formations constituted the dominant form of military tactical formation in eighteenth- and early nineteenth-century European warfare. Linearity thus pervaded both the spatiality of early modern wars and the conceptions of power that they reveal. Linear power *is* coercion: it is the push of one agent's power against the resistance of the other, just as Clausewitz would have us understand by his claim that war is 'an act of force to compel our enemy to do our will'. In linear formations armies confronted one another head on and the exercise of power, just as Hobbes envisaged it in *Leviathan*, is relational and zero-sum. In the modern discourse on war, the augmentation of one side's power necessarily equated the weakening and eventual retreat of the other.

The Battle at Fontenoy on 11 May 1745 amply illustrates the exercise of linear power in war. The French side under Maurice de Saxe stood in formation of an inverted L-shape and were able to withstand assault by both Dutch and British–Hanoverian armies in the protracted War of the Austrian Succession (1740–1748), persevering in the knowledge that the side with the greatest strength would win. Fontenoy was later to stand as de Saxe's greatest triumph, earning him much favour with his political masters. As John Lynn has shown, linear warfare was remarkable in its mirroring of existing ideals and images of the time. It was as if the 'conceptual culture' of the Enlightenment simply migrated top-down from the *philosophes* to the generals.[18] The 'cult of the offensive', which developed in the French army at the end of the eighteenth century and was to last until the First World War, constitutes another, more extreme, manifestation of the conception of linear power in war. As Azar Gat shows, the 'cult of the offensive' or 'doctrine of unconditional offensive', as it is otherwise known, was unique to the French Army at the time.[19] Based on an excessive reliance on firepower, the belief in the cult of the offensive amounted to a belief that whoever strikes first would win. Culminating in the series of futile offensives against Germany of the early days of the First World War, the cult of the offensive ultimately led to massive human cost for France herself: five months into the war France had lost almost a million men, and ten months later the casualties reached one and a half million.[20] The ideal of linear power – power that could be projected straight on the opponent, to linear effect – led to wars with the purpose of physically defeating the enemy, in the first instance by forcing it into retreat and in the second through physical annihilation. This was what successful military leaders did, successfully.

Linear power as projected in warfare reached its apotheosis at the end of the Second World War with the American atomic bombings in Hiroshima and Nagasaki in early August 1945. In Hiroshima, it is estimated that 45,000 people (out of a civilian population of 250,000) died on the first day of the bombings, and a further 19,000 perished in the four months to follow. For Nagasaki, the figures show 22,000 dead on the day of the attack (out of a population of 174,000) and a further 17,000 in the subsequent four months.[21] Deaths of military personnel and foreign workers that went unrecorded at the time add substantially to these figures. With the events of Hiroshima and Nagasaki, it seemed that the projection of power translated into an unlimited unleashing of military force. The modern conception of power seemed finally to have outdone itself as the belief in the linear projection of power to annihilate an enemy had led to the creation of a weapon so potent as to imperil the existence of the planet and humanity as a whole. Thus in *War and the Illiberal Conscience*, Christopher Coker cites as the quintessentially modern manifestation of power the willingness of people 'to commit evil in the name of a greater good', a thoroughly Nietzschean interpretation.[22] (It was in *Beyond Good and Evil* that Nietzsche elaborated on the consequences of a tremendous will to power, predicting a coming 'courage to rechristen our evil as what is best in it'.[23]) In other words, that people 'willed too much' was to become the downfall of modernity: they failed to accept the limits of their own agency.[24] Power became a search for the absolute in modern war and the world suffered the consequences.

The emergence of a nuclear world in the half-century that followed the Second World War highlights the vacillating of the modern mind, not least as regards to the idealisation and imagination of power. The intellectual scaffolding had begun to come down, and the modern conception of power never since inspired the same overzealousness as it did in 1945. Nuclear weapons have not since been put to actual use, yet a system of nuclear deterrence and 'mutually assured destruction' emerged as the world watched, bewildered. Realist writers hailed the bipolar system as one of relative security; yet there was no 'rational calculation' behind what emerged piecemeal and held the world in a grip of fear for the most part. Philip Windsor called the system of nuclear deterrence a form of 'existential suicide', for two reasons: first, the very notion that you can secure the survival of the human race precisely by ensuring its destruction is deeply ironic. Such security is at best a life-denying form of security in which context 'survival itself, and the values that human societies hope to attach to it, lose[s] all meaning'.[25] Second, we have the condemnation of human beings to living with a permanent fear of the future. How could it be expected that any sense of security or freedom is to emanate from such a system? The modern understanding of power as linear, rationally projected force of one party upon another had reached a point of absurdity – and the subtexts of the time began to change irrevocably.

Contrary to theorists of power considered hitherto, Michel Foucault was not concerned with rationalising power, but rather with investigating the effect or functioning of power: the techniques and rationalities of power. Significantly, Foucault insisted that the study of power should move away from questions of sovereignty and legitimacy, and that there was a need to rethink and rearticulate political theory in a way that departed from the modern era's preoccupation with sovereignty, to 'cut off the King's head'.[26] His *Discipline and Punish* (1978) depicts the transition from the Middle Ages' spectacles of public punishment, most graphically illustrated by public hangings, to the 'systematic control of individual members of society' institutionalised with the eighteenth-century development of bureaucratic institutions. One of the most poignant insights that Foucault's earlier work offers to the debate about power and modernity is the view that in order for power to be effective (that is, in order for power to qualify as 'power') those subject to it must be rendered susceptible to its effects.[27] Thus, the modern prison stands as an example of the technique of modern power – a power that, in Foucault's terms, both 'represses and reproduces', *constituting* normalised subjects.[28]

Foucault's decoupling of the analysis of power from that of legitimacy, authority and sovereignty can be seen as indicative of the shift from modern to postmodern conceptualisations of power. Nonetheless, sociologist Gerard Delanty has suggested that we risk overstating the divide between modernity and postmodernity at peril of obscuring the 'radicality of the modern itself'.[29] The question we may legitimately ask is whether assumptions about power's linearity, which informed early notions of political community in the shape of a collective surrendering of power to a sovereign, as well as subsequent formalisation of linear power in the form of the modern bureaucracy, already from the outset contained the seeds of radicality. The potential for total war would certainly suggest so, as would the potency of political ideologies in the modern period. In any event, modern institutional incarnations of linear power have come under attack in recent decades, both in practical and ideational terms.

## Power and politics in a globalised world

'The key problem is no longer to ensure that our social and national systems are *stable*,' wrote Stephen Toulmin, 'rather, it is to ensure that intellectual and social procedures are more *adaptive*.'[30] In his story of how the modern cosmopolis emerged, Toulmin returns to its ultimate foundation: an image of Nature as 'a stable physical system of bodies moving in fixed orbits around a single, central source of power'.[31] Toulmin saw the planetary model of society as explicitly cosmopolitical for 'it generated social relations wherein authority was self-explanatory, self-justifying, and seemingly rational ... both *cosmos* and *polis* (it appeared) were self-contained, and their joint "rationality" guaranteed their stability'.[32] Having dismantled the cosmopolis of the modern era, 'our concern can no longer be to guarantee the stability and uniformity of Science or the State alone: instead, it must be to provide the elbowroom we need in order to protect diversity and *adaptability*'.[33] The quest for adaptability is central to the account of power that sustains the contemporary account of politics and war – imminently visible in the metaphorical imagination of policing wars.

The theme of power as adaptability is ubiquitous and far-reaching in contemporary literature: it recurs in writings as disparate as those of Zygmunt Bauman, Manuel Castells, Steven Lukes, Joseph Nye or Anne-Marie Slaughter. Bauman in his *Liquid Modernity* (2000) identifies 'escape, slippage, elision and avoidance' as the prime techniques of contemporary power. Moreover, he informs us that the exercise of power no longer pertains to static physical control over space (or time), but rather to the ability to control the flow of ideas and mobile 'subjects'.[34] This image clearly contrasts with the linear and hierarchical images of power that dominated the modern era: then power could be 'established', if not with permanent effect, then nevertheless with a degree of stasis. Escape, slippage, elision and avoidance signal the very opposite of static control. Indeed the notion of 'control' appears altogether divorced from power. This absence of control has profound consequences for the way in which politics and political life is conceived: it challenges the modern image of citizens collectively relinquishing power in the hands of an all-powerful sovereign, who is then able to wield that power with citizens' consent. Bauman thus tells the story of a 'fluid milieu', where 'old routines are quickly eroded and new ones have no time to acquire shape', and of a context where 'all action is *experimental*'.[35]

Bauman's exposé constitutes an early account of the limits of power in the contemporary era, and countenancing with 'liquid power' has become a struggle for both theorists and practitioners. Nostalgia for static notions of power still prevails among Western political elites, and while on a theoretical level people may be willing to accept that power simply cannot be 'established' or 'held' in the same way today as in earlier periods, this is a difficult lesson in practical terms, not least for the military. Joseph Nye's influential account of 'soft power' is a good example of such ambivalence in this account, states are no longer capable of establishing power or control over one another: instead, they must aim to influence the actions and behaviour of others through 'softer' means.[36] Nonetheless, the expectation is still that (soft) power can be instrumentally – deliberately – *employed* with the same linear effects as was the case in the modern era. Nye's conviction that soft power can be wielded in the same way today as classic 'hard power' could be during the modern era, and that it would be perceived as *different* from conventional hard power, is noteworthy. Nonetheless, the ambition to combine 'hard' and 'soft' power is evident in various practices of counterinsurgency, including the stated commitment to winning 'hearts and minds' and notions such as the much touted 'clear, hold, build' which gained prominence in the context of the intervention in Iraq.

Manuel Castells' account of the 'new social morphology' in *Information Society* offers an analogous portrait of power in the twenty-first century to that of Bauman.[37] By juxtaposing power and identity Castells effectively illustrates the altered routes and trajectories of power: '... the more a social organization is based upon ahistorical flows, superseding the logic of any one specific place, the more the logic of global power escapes the socio-political control of historically specific local/national societies'.[38] The account that emerges in Castells' trilogy is one of power released from territoriality, flowing instead through networks – a prevalent spatiality of our times, as we saw in Chapter 3. We also saw earlier in this chapter how the waning of modern conceptions of power translated into a disruption of modern institutions founded upon this conception. To the demise of the sovereign nation-state and its chief hierarchical institutions, Castells adds the institutions of schools, Church, hospitals, 'bureaucracies of all kinds'.[39] Castells does not substantively define power but rather describes its ways and means; ultimately, he tells us, 'while there are still power relationships in society, the bypassing of centres of flows of information circulating in networks creates a new, fundamental hierarchy: the power of flows takes precedence over the flows of power'.[40] In other words, Castells' work reveals more about the ontology and epistemology of power than any 'theory' of power could. For this reason it has been immensely influential.

The metaphor of the network has resonated widely over the past decade. Castells himself used it to describe a range of phenomenon from the socio-economic and technological to the ideological. It has been picked up by advisors on American foreign policy such as Anne-Marie Slaughter in search of new ways of projecting American power globally.[41] And of course the network image has found its way into the literature on war, not least through the coining of the term 'network-centric warfare' (NCW).[42] There was for a while much hype around the notion of network-centric war, one suspects not least as it appealed to the technologically minded who had already attained such prominent roles within the US military. By virtue of new technologies information systems could be considerably advanced, leading also to an increased sharing of battlefield information. According to the ideals of NCW, individual soldiers were to be joined in networked structures of robust information sharing, which in turn would generate a common situational awareness. In the image of network-centric war such awareness is thought to improve collaboration, 'self-synchronization' and speed, in turn enhancing mission effectiveness.[43] Indeed, the concept of network-centrism spawned further thinking on the role of the soldier in less directly military terms and generated yet another strategic concept: 'effects-based operations' (EBO). This somewhat tautological term encouraged the military use also of non-military power to achieve desired effects in the target milieu (a quest we shall return to at the end of this chapter).[44]

For all the hype surrounding NCW retired US Navy Admiral Arthur Cebrowski pointed out the most significant 'discovery' of the network-centric warfare debate: 'when you rack and stack all of that, what we are really talking about is a new theory of war, because we are talking of new sources of power'.[45] Power, in Cebrowski's view was no longer a property that could be measured in 'real' terms but rather a something that could 'work or not work': an amorphous and elusive thing. In this vein too, Anne-Marie Slaughter's account of international politics reveals an ontological shift in the conception of power, not (as theorists of 'network politics' or 'network-centric war' may want to argue) simply a new 'substantive theory' of politics or war.

Yet another indication of the omnipresence of the theme of power as adaptability in recent years is the attention given to complexity theory. Previously confined to natural sciences, notably of ecosystems, theories of complexity are increasingly invoked in politics and IR, in the study of *social* systems as well as natural ones – including the study of strategy and war.[46] Christopher Coker has thus imagined states as 'complex adaptive systems' – an image possible only with the shift in understandings of power and politics from a concern with modern static control to the current preoccupation with adaptation and adaptability.[47] The omnipresence of adaptation and adaptability in part responds to the dilemma outlined in Chapter 2: the trapping of agents in a post-teleological world in a radical present where present-day actions demand rationalisation on their own terms, not in relation to past or future. To be effective in this radical present, we are told that power and politics need to be adaptable, fluid and flexible.

Two debates stand out as particularly influential both in terms of the theorising of power and in terms of addressing the relationship of 'war' and 'policing'. The first emerged around Hardt and Negri's notion of 'empire',[48] the key argument of which is that we are living under conditions of global war, albeit a global war controlled – 'policed' – by sovereign power. Power, in Hardt and Negri's view, is thus manifest in a 'new figure of the collective biopolitical body'.[49] The purported 'imperial expansion' that is *empire* has 'nothing to do with imperialism' (as we know it); instead, Hardt and Negri argue, *empire* emerged with the end of modern colonialisms, which in turn 'yielded to new forms of rule that operated on a global scale'.[50] The source of this *empire* is 'a new economic-industrial-communicative machine – (...) a globalized biopolitical machine'.[51] For Hardt and

Negri, politics *is* war, and global capital conspires with the very essence of liberalism to generate not only the will to dominate global relations but also the *capacity* to do so, paving the way for a gigantic biopolitical system where each and every agent is policed – a system, in other words, where control and policing *work*.

Though Hardt and Nergi's argument also rests on the affinities between 'war' and 'policing' in the contemporary age, their argument is substantively different from the one here presented. Hardt and Negri seek to give an account of the politics of the US' world hegemony and its manifest expressions; they tell the story of how US power 'actually' works. In contrast, the argument here presented about a metaphorical imagination of war 'as' policing depicts what appears to be the prevalent view of liberal decision-makers in the post-9-11 era: the view that war *ought* to be a species of policing – that the use of military force by liberal states, through its rationalisation and form is, in fact, order-creating. Whereas the thesis of war as biopolitics finds that control works – that subjects are in fact controlled through a politics of life – the present analysis of the *rationalisation* of war as policing seeks to expose the hollowness and fantasmatic nature of the claim that war is 'order-creating'. Along with the manifold failures of policing wars, *resistance* to policing wars exposes precisely that they do not 'work' (a theme that will be further explored in Chapter 5).

A second influential debate was that which emerged around Giorgio Agamben's *State of Exception* (2005). With this book, Agamben spawned a series of writings on the distinction between peace and war, and the way in which this distinction is challenged by what he sees as a permanent 'state of exception' on the international scene.[53] Like Hardt and Negri, Agamben views liberalism as a totalised power machine, willing and able to dominate the world and reduce it opponents to docile 'subjects'. Thus Agamben's *Homo Sacer* tells the story of liberal power through an analogy with the concentration camp, only this time the concentration camp writ global.[54] In this rendition, the declaration of a war on terror by the United States produced a permanent and global state of exception – the instantiation of Schmitt's sovereign power, suspending all rules. In Agamben's words, 'Bush is attempting to produce a situation in which emergency becomes the rule, and the very distinction between peace and war (and between foreign and civil war) becomes impossible.'[55] Power in

Agamben's account thus remains absolute, confined in the hands of a global sovereign.

Clearly, liberal states' suspension of key liberties in favour of 'security' constitutes a devastating development in recent years as regards the relationship between liberal states, their citizens and citizens of other states. Practices such as extraordinary rendition or illegal detention are rightly the cause of great concern. The point about such practices, however, is precisely that states do *not* broadcast them; instead, they are kept out of the spotlight as much as possible. The Obama administration's expansion of drone attacks follows precisely this trajectory: the practice is downplayed, and debate is kept at bay through the insistence that the attacks constitute a minimal part of the general approach to the use of force. Thus, the policing wars narrative presents these practices as precisely 'exceptional', while the remainder of the narrative constructs the use of military force as part of 'normal' politics, the everyday mundane necessity of upholding 'order' and pursuing 'disorderly' elements, be they 'criminals' or 'terrorists'.

The assumptions and ideals that underpin the metaphor of war as policing are the product of a specific set of circumstances, where images of time, space, power and agency play key parts in constructing a collective imagination of social phenomena. The two final sections of this chapter turn to the ways in which conceptions of power have led to ideal notions of how power 'should' operate in contemporary wars. Two features of the liberal discourse on war as it relates to power stand out: first, the belief that it is possible to effect a 'transfer of power' through war – from the intervening forces to the local ones; and second, the adjacent belief that such a transfer of power will be matched by a 'transfer of authority', similarly from the intervening forces to the local. Both these facets testify to the way in which 'power as adaptability' has surpassed the linear imagination of power that dominated the early modern period.

### The 'transfer of power': building local forces in Iraq and Afghanistan

The invasion of Afghanistan in 2001 had an immediate impetus and initially a singular objective: to topple the Taliban regime and, to capture or kill Osama bin Laden himself. As we saw in the discussion of the end of decisiveness in war (Chapter 2), the objectives of the international forces in Afghanistan have since evolved considerably – to a point where the question 'what are we doing in Afghanistan?' appeared perfectly ordinary even in mainstream American and European debates.[56] The situation in Iraq followed a similar trajectory whereby the lack of strategic objective initially was attributed to 'poor post-invasion planning' but later was shown to be endemic to the intervention itself. Under conditions of a radical present, there is a marked tendency for present-day actions not to be instrumentally rationalised, defended or explained in relation to a distant utopian goal.[57] For this reason Bauman's reference to 'experimental action' is particularly apt: objectives are constantly articulated and re-articulated in terms that are intended to make present-day action legitimate on its own terms. For Bauman, these 'reconnaissance battles' are the most common category of warfare in a 'global frontierland'.[58] This radical presentism is, as we shall see, fundamentally linked to the idealised notions of how power operates most effectively in the contemporary, globalised world.

With the adoption of UN Security Council Resolution 1546 in June 2004, the international community formally restored sovereignty to the people of Iraq by formally ending the occupation of the country by the US-led coalition, which since March 2003 had ruled the country through the Coalition Provisional Authority (CPA).[59] But the attempted 'transferral of sovereignty' was in a sense always hypothetical. As a result of the policy of 'de-Baathification' adopted by L. Paul Bremer, the American administrator of Iraq under the CPA in November 2003, very little remained of Iraqi governing structures. De-Baathification had as its purpose the removal of former members of Saddam Hussein's Baath party and ordered the dismissal of all senior government officials as well as the dissolution of Iraq's 500,000-member military and intelligence service.[60] Iraq had no functioning police or military to speak of at the time, and consequently no means of practically upholding its newfound sovereignty.

In part, this reflects a familiar dissonance: sovereignty always has an internal and an external dimension, the former building on the idea of a social contract between citizens and state and the latter a reflection of the state's capacity to exercise that sovereign power externally. Another way of conceptualising the different dimensions of classical sovereignty lies in the difference between its *de jure* and its *de facto* qualities: the former signifying the recognition of a state's juridical status as sovereign and the latter the actual capacity of the government in question to exercise such control. In post-invasion Iraq, however, the gap between expectations and aspirations was wider than common definitions allow. There was little basis in terms of the internal policies of Iraq: no elections had been held at the time, and there seemed to be a distinct lack of a social contract between the interim government in place and the population. Instead, the way in which the interim government was assembled (a process that began with the formation of the Iraqi Governing Council in 2003) seemed to reflect the political priorities of the coalition members more than it did the actual conditions in Iraq.[61] Above all, the fact that the US-led coalition could effectively decide when sovereignty was to be restored to Iraq by renouncing its occupation testifies to the tied political situation. The UN Security Council essentially faced a choice of either tacitly endorsing a continued occupation of the country (politically unfeasible given the lack of a UN mandate for the invasion in the first place), or endorsing the end of the occupation and Iraq's newfound sovereign status. That this sovereign status was in name only, and that more than a hundred thousand international troops were in the midst of fighting a war in the country, had little sway over the preconceived view that a 'transfer of sovereignty' should be possible.

The establishment of national security forces, police, military and intelligence, over the years emerged a central priority for the international community in both Iraq and Afghanistan. The goal of building functioning police and military was re-stated on numerous occasions by various representatives of the intervening forces in each context, and survived transition of political leadership in both the United States and Britain. The final communiqué from the International Conference on Afghanistan held in London in January 2010 stipulated the need for Afghan national forces to take over responsibility for the security situation as soon as possible, and the withdrawal of international troops in 2014 was hinged on the successful 'handover' to local security forces.[62] In Iraq the CPA in 2004 proclaimed the task of raising new security forces for Iraq a key element of its strategy for stemming the increasing levels of violence in the country.[63] In both Afghanistan and Iraq, the task of building local forces was presented as *intrinsic* to the war effort and stood at the very epicentre of an 'exit strategy' for the international forces; as such, it testifies to the integration of war-fighting with broader civilian aims. Security Sector Reform (SSR) programmes, when carried out alongside large-scale military interventions epitomise this logic.[64] A successful transfer of power has been advocated both for the sake of the states in question and for the sake of the international community that is seeking to terminate its engagement. The fate of the attempt to build new police and military forces in Afghanistan and Iraq in turn offers important clues as to how the policing discourse on war is sustained by particular conceptions of power.

Foucault's account of the destructive and productive nature of power simultaneously describes the function of power at the height of the modern period and prefigures its demise.[65] Gone are the days of absolute control; no longer do Panoptical structures lend themselves to the exercise of complete control of subjects through constant observation. No longer are the people in charge, those exercising power, 'there', so to speak; no longer do they occupy seats 'in the controlling tower'.[66] There are few possibilities for hierarchical and linear control in the early twenty-first century, and war is no exception. As might have been expected, the idea that sovereignty in Iraq after the invasion could simply be *transferred back* to the Iraqi population did not easily translate into practice. Rather than the linear control pertaining both to classic notions of sovereignty and to the exercise of military power in modern wars, the attempt to 'transfer power' in Iraq or Afghanistan seems to sidestep linear power altogether. Instead, in these settings, both the notion of sovereignty and the exercise of military power have come to reflect a *dissipation* and *dispersal* of control. The notion that power is a quality or possession that can be readily transferred from one agent to another is suggestive of deep-seated tension in the shift from modern linear conceptions of power to power as adaptability, central to contemporary social and political life. Indeed, COIN FM 3–24 posits adaptability as the key trait of successful counterinsurgency: 'in COIN, the side that learns faster and adapts more rapidly – the better learning organisation – usually wins', we are told, and *Learn and Adapt* is promptly identified as a key imperative for US forces.[67] The relationship between power and politics, neatly tied together in the modern imagination, is fraught in the twenty-first century: power no longer operates in a linear fashion, and therefore politics cannot be straightforwardly conjectured either. If the techniques of power are 'avoidance, slippage and elision', as Bauman claims, it should come as no surprise that the ambition to 'transfer power' has met much resistance in both Iraq and Afghanistan.

Seemingly confirming Bauman's notion of all action being 'experimental action', the establishment of new national police and military forces was not articulated as a goal from the outset of the wars in either Iraq or Afghanistan. In Iraq the task was assumed virtually by default, as a consequences of the lapse into violence and criminality in 2003, which took the occupying forces largely by surprise. As a result of the lack of political priority given to the task, much of the work was initially outsourced to international private military/security companies. The task of training the new Iraqi police force was awarded to DynCorp International under an 'infinite quantity, infinite delivery' contract, while Vinnell Corporation was assigned responsibility for training of the new Iraqi armed forces.[68] The haphazard way in which the task of building up military and police forces was undertaken in the early days of the Iraq war became a source of much criticism in the years to follow, as the training of Iraq police and military began to be awarded higher priority.

Afghanistan followed a similar trajectory of sovereignty formally restored in the midst of war. Yet from his appointment at the International Conference on Afghanistan held in Bonn in 2001, to his re-election in the fraudulent elections held in August 2009, President Hamid Karzai and his government failed to exert authority in the country. And so too in Afghanistan, the effort to 'transfer power' from the US-led forces to local police and military yielded feeble results. The Afghan National Party (ANP) has suffered problems of recruitment, illiteracy, widespread drug abuse and corruption fuelled by undiminished opium production.[69] Similar complaints are made of the Afghan National Army (ANA), which also suffers high rates of attrition.[70] Not least are there significant issues of trust between ANP or ANA and the local population: more often than not, citizens view the police as a source of fear rather than a source of security. The dramatic increase in what has been dubbed 'green on blue fire' – Afghan security forces attacking ISAF (International Security Assistance Force) troops – since 2009 show the vacuity of the 'handing over authority' mantra. The programme launched to double the size of the Afghan army in 2009, with ISAF support, seems to have ushered in precisely the opposite trajectory as massive recruitment took place among disillusioned young Afghans, often mourning the loss of relatives at the hand of NATO forces. The attempt to portray the 'green on blue' incidents, which sharply increased in 2012, as the unfortunate consequence of 'Taliban infiltration' illustrates the level of desperation that has entered the mainstream policing narrative.[71]

The attempt to construct functioning national security forces is not a task divergent from the war effort, an isolated state-building task. On the contrary, it emerged an integral part of the war effort; indeed effecting a 'transfer of power' through the building of local forces *became* war. For the US-led forces both in Iraq and Afghanistan, it is a crucial component of counterinsurgency strategy. Under US auspices the Afghan National Police have been encouraged to operate as a counterinsurgency force, testifying to a general militarisation of police in the country.[72] The prestige invested in a successful 'transfer of power' by the international community has not been lost on opponents to ISAF forces, and the new police and military forces have become 'battlegrounds' in their own right. In Iraq, more than 700 police recruits were killed in insurgent attacks in the first year alone.[73] In many cases, suicide attacks were carried out against gatherings of people simply lining up to apply; they never made it to police status.[74] Similarly, the Afghan National Police suffered extremely high rates of attack, and have been gauged three times more likely to be killed than soldiers in the Afghan army.[75]

The goals for a purported transfer of power have been set to a high level in the case of Afghanistan. In 2009 a force of 134,000 Afghan military and 82,000 police had been created, and aims were set by the United States at the creation of a combined security forces (military, police and intelligence) of between 400,000 and 500,000 – a high figure for a country with a population of 33 million.[76] Forces on this scale have no fiscal basis in Afghanistan: the cost of maintaining security forces of such numbers has been estimated at $2 billion to $3 billion/year, whereas the annual revenue of the Afghan government not more than $600 million in 2009;[77] the irony of developing countries being criticised for spending 30 percent of their budget on defence while Afghanistan is being encouraged to spend 500 percent of its budget on security is startling.[78] The intervening forces' consistently expanding estimates of the required number of security forces testify not simply to the magnitude of the task, but to the impossibility of overcoming inherent contradictions in the narrative itself.

The prevalence of international private security companies that effectively crowd out the building of state forces further testifies to such contradictions: in the effort to 'transfer power' from one set of forces (international) to another (local), they constitute a pull on potential recruits, offering better work conditions and salaries many times higher than offered by the state.[79] In Iraq the boom of the international private security industry generated much debate after it was estimated that international PSC (private security contractors) staff in the country totalled 20,000 in 2004, thus outnumbering British forces and constituting the second largest foreign contingent after the Americans.[80] Efforts have since been made for the Iraqi government to exercise control over which companies are permitted to operate in the country, but this has only been partially effective.[81] By comparison, the astounding level of international PSC activity in Afghanistan has gone largely unnoticed: at the end of 2009 an Afghan government official estimated that there were 60,000 personnel employed by international PSCs in the country, over which the government exercised very little influence.[82]

Moreover, while the stated goal is the transfer of power to government structures in both locations, efforts have also been made to build up parallel structures of security. The overt and covert sponsoring of local militias has occupied a central part in the strategic effort, from the 'Sons of Iraq' to the 'Afghan National Police Auxiliary', a militia force created by the United States for 'community policing' in southern Afghanistan in 2006, and the later Afghanistan Public Protection Force Programme (APPF), intended as a 'village self-defence forces'.[83] Together with the prominent role of international PSCs in both Iraq and Afghanistan, the financing of private local militias constitute a pull in the opposite direction to the purportedly sought 'transfer of power' and suggest that faith in the task of transferring power (as capacity) from international to local forces may be waning also on the part of the international forces. In recognition of the fraught and contradictory process, the US Special Representative to Afghanistan and Pakistan, Richard Holbrooke, acknowledged in December 2009 that institution-building in Afghanistan would have to start 'from scratch' in the ninth year of engagement.[84]

Evidently, modern conceptions of power as linear capacity still linger in the imagination of decision-makers as the paradigmatic understanding of how power translates into political effect. Modelled on the European development of strong states in the seventeenth and eighteenth centuries, the assumption of 'capacity-building' is that power can be fostered by the international community as an integral part of war, and then readily conferred upon local forces.[85] The futile attempt to reconcile linear power with a new subtext of power, flowing through amorphous networks, skirting around the themes of adaptability and elision, has foundered in the convoluted narrative of policing war. A final irony of the attempted 'transfer of power' in Afghanistan is the failure to prevent or counter the establishment of shadow state structures by the Taliban. Alternative structures of 'law and order' including governors, police chiefs, district administrators and judges have been set up in most provinces around the country, including Kandahar, Gardez, Ghazni and Laghman province.[86] In the Laghman province the Taliban shadow governor, Maulvi Shaheed Khail, reportedly issued edicts on stationery of the 'Islamic Republic of Afghanistan' (the Taliban's official name).

The idea of lean 'capacity-building' has been criticised for being overly technical, and for promoting hard, physical power of local forces at the expense of democratic accountability and good governance more broadly conceived. In an attempt to conjoin power and legitimacy of new security forces, the international debate shifted perceptibly from the emphasis on 'capacity' to one of 'authority' as the intervention was nearing the end of a decade's engagement. The pledge to create trusted authority in the midst of ongoing war is a step further into the heart of the domestic politics of target states such as Iraq or Afghanistan, as the final section of this chapter will argue. Its purchase is not surprising, however: the belief that authority, like power, should be a property that can be obtained by external forces and then 'transferred' to local ones has become integral to the currently immensely popular strategy of counterinsurgency.

### The 'transfer of authority' and the chimera of counterinsurgency

Prior to the wars in Afghanistan and Iraq, the United States had distanced itself from protracted military ventures – a process that began with the withdrawal of American troops from its intervention in Somalia in 1992–1994 after the killing of eighteen American soldiers. On its entry into office in 2000, the second Bush administration was bent on avoiding the complex operations of Somalia, Haiti, the Balkans and elsewhere. The change over the last decade could hardly be greater: from a time when so called 'complex operations' were rather dismissively referred to as MOOTW – 'military operations other than war' – a remarkable change of heart has taken place within the US military.[87] Key strategic documents such as the *Quadrennial Defense Reviews* of 2006 and 2010 established counterinsurgency as the paradigmatic operation of the present as well as medium- to long-term future for the US military.[88] COIN became the word on everyone's lips, and the race to perfect its practice was on.

Inspired by the perceived success of General Petraeus' surge in Iraq, US General Stanley A. McChrystal issued his assessment of the situation Afghanistan in August 2009, suggesting a similar surge in military capacity of 30,000 additional American troops.[89] McChrystal's strategy underlined three core principles of COIN in Afghanistan: the protection of the Afghan people, the building of Afghan government capabilities and the instruction to soldiers to make friends with whomever they can. Pursuing members of the Taliban and other insurgents was deemed to be of secondary importance for US and ISAF soldiers as the object of 'protecting the population' was articulated as the top priority for US-led forces in Afghanistan.[90]

David Kilcullen's influence on American counterinsurgency is noteworthy for his insistence on the importance of perceptions: it does not matter whether US forces 'win' an encounter of any scale unless they are perceived as winning by the opposing side: in Kilcullen's words, 'political perception matters more than battlefield success'.[91] For this reason, he instructs militaries to control the 'message' conveyed: every single soldier should be mindful of the 'global audience' watching them through global and instantaneous media.[92] Since Barack Obama assumed office in 2009, the emphasis on 'communication' as part of counterinsurgency strategy has increased dramatically (a topic that will be further explored in Chapter 5), bringing the narrative of war metaphorically as policing to its logical extreme.

On the British side, the re-examination of strategic thinking captured in the Defence White Paper of 2003 highlighted the networking of forces (in a bid to develop a British alternative to the American network-centric warfare, calling it instead 'network-enabled capability', NEC), an 'effects-based approach to operations' (EBAO) and the centrality of 'modular expeditionary forces'.[93] When a new British doctrine of 'stabilisation operations' (JDP 3–40) was published at the end of 2009, it followed seamlessly from the 'comprehensive approach' of 2006.[94] The 'comprehensive approach' in turn was inspired by a broadened understanding of security, beyond physical security, which had been circling in European foreign policy debates since Javier Solana's European Security Strategy (ESS) of 2003.[95] The ESS reflected the conviction that contemporary security problems were complex: security and development could not be separated from one another, and security problems therefore demand a high level of proficiency in relations between civilian and military agencies.[96] Calls for a 'civilian surge' to accompany the military one in Afghanistan testified to a widespread acceptance of and call for a more integrated military–civilian effort than ever previously.[97]

The assembling of all tasks into a 'comprehensive whole' that gives equal consideration to physical security, social and economic development, environmental sustainability, identity politics and so on is seductive: it is difficult to argue with an approach that promises to be 'holistic'. So seductive in fact, that under the narrative of the comprehensive approach it is difficult to remember that military intervention still involves war-fighting. This is at the heart of the policing metaphor, of course: the notion that war somehow is no longer 'war' but the creation of a specific type of order. When the 2009 British strategy for Afghanistan used the following terms: 'International ... regional ... joint civilian–military ... co-ordinated ... long-term ... focused on developing capacity ... an approach that combines respect for sovereignty and local values with respect for international standards of democracy, legitimate and accountable government, and human rights; a hard-headed approach: setting clear and realistic objectives with clear metrics of success' it stood as ample evidence of the level of wishful thinking among policy makers.[98] However earnest the widening of security ambitions from physical security to economic, social, identity and even psychological security – which through the concept of 'human security' in the late 1990s foreshadowed the emergence of a policing metaphor of war – the realisation that reality might demand a prioritisation between these aims blighted policymakers.[99] The warning of the then NATO Secretary General, Jaap de Hoop Scheffer, that 'places like Afghanistan cannot be divided up into neat spheres of responsibility for peacekeeping, combat operations and reconstruction' led him to conclude that 'the country will be won or lost in its entirety'.[100] To admit the latter as a conclusion to NATO's involvement in Afghanistan is anathema to Western decision-makers; endless war is the logical progression.

While shifts in strategic thinking as regards COIN in both US and UK military circles were related to the situations in Iraq and Afghanistan, the basic tenets of the emerging consensus have deeper roots. They reflect the metaphorical image of war as an order-creating force. COIN thinking is thus the most recent instantiation of the policing metaphor into concrete strategies, doctrines and operational guidelines. In wars underpinned by postmodern conceptions of power as adaptability, the objective can no longer be to *win* but only to manage change: to create and maintain order – as one would expect of a police force. As Theo Farrell and Stuart Gordon point out, it is the *consent* of the population that is sought in current counterinsurgency operations in Iraq or Afghanistan.[101] As we saw earlier, the notion of consent was central to the modern conceptualisation of power as authority. Faith in the techniques of 'adapatability', 'evasion' or 'slippage' thus comes up against reluctance to let go of the modern ideal of linear power as capacity and the established rendition of consent and 'authority'. It is thus possible to detect a similar ambivalence over conceptions of power to that we saw over postmodern conceptions of space/spatiality in the previous chapter. Interestingly, Paul Cornish refers to the comprehensive approach precisely as 'elusive'.[102] It would seem that such elusiveness constitutes part of the explanation for the appeal of these ideas.

The contradictions of COIN are inherent in the quest to align warfighting with the creation of 'governance', 'authority' and even 'trust'. General David D. McKiernan, then Commander of the ISAF forces in Afghanistan, admitted in 2009 to a lack of popular trust in the Karzai government.[103] Yet, however scant support for the government in question may be, support to the host government cannot be eliminated from the broader counterinsurgency effort as it is presently articulated. Indeed, the very basis for the legitimacy of the prolonged presence of international forces in both Iraq and Afghanistan remains the notion that they are there to support the governments in respective place. Were this relationship to break down, securing a UN mandate for the international troops would hardly be conceivable: it would too closely resemble occupation, and the only alternative would be for the states in question to become full-scale UN protectorates, in the vein of Kosovo or East Timor. In other words, there appears to be little hope of untangling the contradictions of 'counterinsurgency war to build trust'; rather, they are reflections of inherent tensions in the metaphorical understanding of war as order-creating, indeed as 'policing'.

Populations in both Iraq and Afghanistan continue to profess a high level of distrust for the new police and military forces, albeit for somewhat different reasons. Whereas in the case of Afghanistan, perceptions of incompetence and erraticness on the part of the police appear the foremost reason for the population's distrust, Iraqi citizens seem to fear a police force that is beginning to be all too effective, and some hint at the establishment of a new police state (in the conventional sense of the word) in Iraq.[104] Beyond a general sense of disbelief among local populations, concrete manifestations of the contradictions between 'breaking things and killing people', which militaries are traditionally known to do, and 'creating order' stand out. Consider the issue of force protection, keenly prioritised by the international forces. The irony of placing such emphasis on protection of the international forces in the context of striving to effect lasting change in Afghanistan is not lost on the general population. A piece of anecdotal evidence illustrates this well: a man interviewed by Swedish national news media on the streets of Mazar-i Sharif in northern Afghanistan, the area where the Swedish troops are deployed, was asked whether he did not agree that, at the very least, the presence of the international troops allowed people like him the security to walk on the streets. To this the man replied, laughingly: 'No, it is because there are people like *me* on the streets that *your troops* can feel safe here!'[105]

The attempt by international military and civilian implementers to construct 'legitimate authority' in a state whose political culture they do not understand is fraught to say the least, as evidenced by the widespread incidence of what by Western standards is 'corruption'. In Afghan society, for instance, the levels of trust may rather understandably be higher between individuals with long-standing family ties than between individuals belonging to historically rival groups, forced to work together as a result of an international military intervention.[106] In the final analysis, a transfer of authority through counterinsurgency warfare appears chimerical for the reason that we ultimately cannot *will* anything on behalf of another. It may be possible to transfer concrete matters or even abilities, but it is not possible to do the same with political persuasion. The will to create and maintain civil order is not part of the category of 'transferables'. One Western official's impression of the general Afghan reaction to the question is instructive. His understanding of the general Afghan opinion was that it seemed to say: 'we never handed you authority in the first place, so how could you ever give it "back"'?'[107] In this context, the ambition not to *win* but to 'understand and persuade' is woefully unrealistic.[108]

## Conclusion: war and the struggle over power

An understanding of power is intrinsic to any understanding of war and an essential component of any discourse on war. Preconceptions about power, its nature and function, inevitably influence our understanding of political action and what it can achieve; and the insight that 'power' and 'war' are phenomenologically linked has led to different interpretations of the relationship between the two over time. This chapter began with an analysis of the modern ideals of power: the notion of power as a linear force, possible to wield instrumentally to desired effects, and examined the way in which such understandings of power laid the foundations for modern social and political thought. Linear conceptions of power were found to have inspired the linear use of force, with wars amenable to decisive victory through the crushing of an enemy under overwhelming physical force. The Second World War was the apotheosis of this type of war: it epitomised the horrific degree to which the Western world had managed to transform its power into outright force through the construction and use of the atomic bomb.

Power in the twenty-first century appears to operate along different lines: power has become ubiquitous and its techniques – in Bauman's rendition, techniques of elision, avoidance and slippage – do not easily lend themselves to political action. As a consequence of altered conceptualisations of power, the intellectual scaffolding that sustains narratives of war has also been transformed. The ambition of 'transferring power' constitutes precisely the kind of objective demanded of protagonists of war living in the absolute present tense. Under conditions of radical presentism, when the means of war appear more important than its ends, decision-makers are hard pressed to choose objectives that can be legitimated on their own terms, *as ends in themselves and not simply as means to an end*. The question of whether these strategies work – whether either a transfer of power or a transfer of authority can in fact be attained – seems to be relegated to being of secondary importance.

The current discourse on war is based on notions of power as a property that can be possessed, transferred and transformed into 'authority'. Such ideals arose out of the assumptions and predispositions of the early modern period. In a world where even the mightiest military force in the world cannot achieve decisive results in the wars it is engaged in, where power seems to flow supraterritorially and where a strong conviction might be a more potent asset than physical power, the ideals of linear power appear increasingly fraught. Neither power nor authority can be readily 'transferred'; yet the liberal world persists in the belief that it can. It does so because this belief constitutes an important part of the way in which the liberal world understands itself, its place in the world and ultimately the wars in which it is currently engaged.

Another set of ideals and preconceptions that constitute a significant part of the explanation for the attractiveness of the policing metaphor will be discussed in the next and final chapter, concerned with contemporary imaginations of political agency.

# 5
# On Agency: Policing Logics and War 'Without Antagonism'

## Introduction

No discourse on war emerges out of a vacuum: it gains resonance as a consequence of its constitutive ideals, preconceptions and values fitting with the structure of key social imaginaries. The theme of this chapter – agency – is itself a theme of liberal thought with its lead motifs of *inter alia* liberty, freedom of choice, equality among men before the law and so on. The subjects of liberalism, agency and internationalism constitute an amalgamation of strands that have been alluded to in previous chapters: here we zoom in on the relationship between *law, politics, war* and *policing* – a four-way relationship that constitutes the backbone of the metaphorical understanding of war as policing. The first part of the chapter will discuss how a liberal heritage can be seen to inform the contemporary discourse on war as 'order-creating'. The eschewing of strong foundations in moral and ethical reasoning has thus not forged an abandonment of ideological claims, as is sometimes inferred, but rather new ways of expressing and justifying such claims.

The second purpose of this chapter is to link the discussion of why the metaphor of war as policing is part of a liberal discourse on war to an exposé of 'politics' and 'political agency'. Much as the discussions of time/temporality, space/spatiality and conceptions of power explained specific dimensions of the discourse on 'policing wars', an account of how 'agency' and 'politics' are collectively imagined will provide insight into the origins of the policing metaphor and give further reason for its widespread purchase among decision-makers and analysts in recent years. Finally, 'liberal internationalism' and the exceptional position it has occupied in global debates since the late 1990s, and its relationship with the policing discourse on war, will be discussed.

## Liberal origins of the policing metaphor

Liberalism has had formidable influence philosophically and politically for over three centuries. Through the writings of John Stuart Mill, John Locke, Friedrich Hayek, Karl Popper, and more recently, John Rawls, Brian Barry and Ronald Dworkin, liberal values have been moulded and re-moulded. Meanwhile, what has been understood as 'liberal practices' has changed too. The metaphorical understanding of war as policing is a recent incarnation of liberal values, a current outlook on liberal values operationalised in a particular way. Like the discourse on war, the tradition of liberalism has evolved over time; the evolution of liberalism has both followed and instigated changes in the way is collectively imagined and idealised.

The twentieth century became known as the century of ideological fervour. Yet, as Tzvetan Todorov shows, for all its zealousness, the religiously inspired use of ideology predates the twentieth century.[1] Among the first to discover the radical potential of ideology was Nicholas de Condorcet, who pointed to 'a new danger' for individual autonomy in its potential conflict with collective autonomy at the time of the French Revolution.[2] The conflict between the individual and the collective later would later come to manifest itself as the collective forcing 'redemption' on the individual in the twentieth century.[3] In the early days of the Enlightenment period, this conflict was less apparent. Individual freedom stood as the model of popular sovereignty, and the relationship between individual and collective agency was thus regarded as one of continuity.[4] During the 1920s, before the rise and consolidation of the totalitarian regimes of Europe and Russia, astute observers began to warn again of the 'political religions'. Waldemar Gurion, scholar of totalitarianism, noted the irony of calling explicitly secular ideologies 'religious' and proposed the term 'ideocracy' to signal the religious quality that political ideologies seemed prone to.[5] When commitment to ideology increased, it translated into the most drastic and draconian of social experiments: the Nazi concentration camps and the Gulag stand out as the most gruesome examples of how individual autonomy was trampled in favour of collective agency. At the height of modernity, individuals no longer conceived of any limits to human agency; and this prioritisation of individualism emerged as a plague of the modern imagination. To John Gray, then, the real legacy of the Enlightenment is a world 'ruled by calculation and wilfulness which is humanly unintelligible and destructively purposeless'.[6]

Laurence Freedman deems wars 'liberal' when they are waged for 'liberal ends', when 'force [is] used in pursuit of essentially liberal values'.[7] In line with this reasoning, we find decision-makers' desire to list the values that contemporary wars are said to pursue and promote, such as freedom from oppression, the protection of human rights, a right to self-determination and so on. Some of the reasoning in legal and ethical debates about war depends on this type of argument – the intentions of an agent are presumed to matter, and to be of consequence in determining whether an act (of war) is legal/ethical/moral or, in this case, 'liberal'. The problem in taking this route in explaining why certain wars are appropriately described as liberal or, indeed, why the policing discourse should be seen as belonging to a tradition of liberal wars, is the familiar difficulty of proving 'genuine' intentions behind actions. Whenever the claim is made that wars are being pursued *in the name of such and such value*, we are faced with the difficult issue of how to prove that these are in fact genuine aims of a specific instance of the use of force. This line of reasoning is vulnerable in particular to objections about hypocrisy and double standards, or protests that the 'real reason' behind a decision or event is not revealed.[8]

Three features of liberal thought will be discussed in the section to follow: first, the Enlightenment legacy of universalism and humanism that gave birth to the modern liberal tradition; second, liberalism's faith in law as an instrument in the creation of justice; and third, the contested relationship between liberalism and politics, or between liberalism and 'the political'. In each instance, clues will be given as to why we have arrived at assumptions and ideals that together constitute an idea of war, metaphorically, as policing, and what makes this discourse a distinctly liberal one.

### Humanism and universalism in liberal thought

In outlining the distinctiveness of Enlightenment thinking, Todorov insists on an irreducible humanism:

> the end purpose of freed human deeds, ... was, in its turn, brought down to earth and focused on human beings rather than on God.

In this sense, the Enlightenment was a form of humanism, or, if one prefers, a form of anthropocentrism. It was no longer considered necessary, as theologians had maintained, to always be willing to sacrifice the love of creatures for the love of the Creator: it was henceforth enough to love other human beings.[9]

Such faith in human beings' innate capacity for reason, independent of God, was directly derived from a corresponding faith in human nature and human capacity to do good, a view that simultaneously constituted a rejection of the hitherto dominant Christian view of human nature as flawed. Susan Neiman in her *Evil in Modern Thought* (2004) traces the history of thought on human nature and our capacity for evil, showing how Immanuel Kant and other Enlightenment thinkers considered human capacity for ill ('unreason') a theological question, not a philosophical one. As a consequence, Neiman tells us, theological questions have been 'off limits' for philosophy since Kant argued that 'God (along with other subjects of classical metaphysics) exceeded the limits of human knowledge'.[10] Thus the 'post-Christian' Enlightenment view of human nature de-emphasised its flaws and emphasised human beings' capacity for reason. In his *Critique of Pure Reason* Kant wrote that we have to cast aside knowledge of God in order to create space for faith in human beings' innate capacity for moral improvement.[11]

The commitment to morality acquired mythical qualities in the modern period; and outstanding faith in human capacity for reason would become a hallmark of modern thought. Philosopher Leszek Kolakowski has described the modern desire to see humanity as being on the path of moral progress as follows:

[T]he yearning to be rooted in a world organized by myth aims at defining oneself in a given and experienced order of values; it is a desire to step outside oneself into an order in which one treats oneself as an object within a designated sphere of possibilities ... [I]t is clear that independently of possible personal particularizations to which myth is subject at each absorption by an individual, it can be absorbed by that individual only when he gives it a universally valid, generally binding, and universally human meaning.[12]

The ideals and preconceptions that constitute the liberal discourse on war as policing carry forward important aspects of the Enlightenment version of humanism. The very idea that war can be used as an instrument for re-ordering society through the establishment of law and order and trust between citizens stems from the a priori assumption that human beings are perfectable through their capacity for reason and rational judgement.

The policing metaphor can also be seen to be of liberal descent in its aspiration to universality. While the heyday of teleological certainty is in the past, liberalism's aspiration to universality still prevails. Political theorist Paul Kelly in his recent survey of, and normative argument for, egalitarian liberalism in the twenty-first century is adamant about this. 'Liberals', Kelly tells us, 'are universalists and not particularists, even if some such as Rawls and Dworkin seem to veer toward a kind of particularism. Liberal values are supposed to have a resonance and claim on all humans, wherever they happen to be.'[13] Thus, the disagreement between liberals of communitarian and cosmopolitan convictions respectively is both revealing and obscuring.[14] It is therefore possible to compare the reasoning of Brian Barry – who writes of Enlightenment liberalism as a 'fighting creed' armed with universalist assumptions – with that of Michael Walzer, who advocates 'self-restraint' in liberals' universalist aspirations, restricting themselves to moral minimalism (thinness).[15] Even pragmatist liberals such as Richard Rorty, whose ethical claims are made without recourse to strong foundations, aspire to universalism in his faith in the possibility for a secular, humanist and liberal culture.[16] The individualist, rationalist belief in the possibility of universal consensus based on reason, in other words, appears endemic to liberal thought.[17]

The ideals underpinning the policing discourse bear the imprints of both humanism and universalism. Indeed, the two cannot they be neatly separated from one another: wars continue to be rationalised in terms of the *betterment* of human life, in the ambition of conferring greater happiness on human kind. Tony Blair's notion of a 'battle of global values' is typical:

> We will not win the battle against global extremism unless we win it at the level of values as much as that of force. We can win only by showing that our values are stronger, better, and more just than the alternative. That also means showing the world that we are even-handed and fair in our application of those values. ... It is the age-old battle between progress and reaction, between

those who embrace the modern world and those who reject its existence – between optimism and hope, on the one hand, and pessimism and fear, on the other.[18]

The reasons given for going to war are advocated by liberals as having universal purchase also in the twenty-first century, with the rationale for that all human beings seek the same thing – freedom, happiness, the fulfilment of life under conditions of liberal democracy, and so on – and that this can, in fact, be attained in conjunction with the use of military force. Blair made his case for war on Iraq to the House of Commons in March 2003 thus:

> It is dangerous if such regimes disbelieve us. Dangerous if they think they can use our weakness, our hesitation, even the natural urges of our democracy towards peace, against us. Dangerous because one day they will mistake our innate revulsion against war for permanent incapacity; when in fact, pushed to the limit, we will act. But then when we act, after years of pretence, the action will have to be harder, bigger, more total in its impact.[19]

The policing metaphor is heir also to the link established in modern thought between morality and 'rationality', above all, the notion that morality is something we can achieve through reason. This was the aspect of modern thought most deplored by Nietzsche, who saw it as evidence of the Enlightenment containing the seeds of its own destruction. Nihilism would be the result of this misplaced intermingling of morality and rationality, Nietzsche warned.[20] In his attack on contemporary liberalism, Gray finds this nihilism in the process of being globalised:

> Nothing remains of this project but the expansion of human productive powers through the technological domination of the earth. It is this conjunction of the global spread of the Western humanist project with the self-understanding of its most powerful modern embodiment in the Enlightenment that warrants the claim that we find ourselves now at the close of the modern age.[21]

On the one hand, the ideals and preconceptions that underpin the contemporary understanding of war are largely based on the Enlightenment legacy of humanism and universalism. On the other

hand, we have seen the power of liberal 'faith' weakened by the dis-
enchantment produced by the events of the twentieth century: two
world wars, the rise of totalitarianism, exterminations, camps, and
finally fifty years of superpower stand-off that held a whole world
hostage. Ideologies no longer hold the power to compel or inspire
conviction of a religious kind. In this respect, Tony Blair is perhaps
the exception to the rule. Indeed, it could be said that he failed to
elicit more support for his views precisely because of the level of
conviction he demonstrated: to the unconvinced, there seemed to be
something suspect about a man of such persuasion.

The weakened humanism that we see evidence of in the understanding of war as an instrument in the creation of order can be
seen as an attempt to mitigate disenchanted, postmodern nihilism.
Decision-makers appear unhappy with their status as risk managers
and, wanting something other than reflexivity to live by, they do still
invoke values. In this context, the ascending status of law in recent
decades has played a prominent role. As fewer people find themselves capable of expressing moral or ethical certitude, holding on to
the law has become a method of choice for many. When Gray raises
the question of whether 'the theoretical goal of the new liberalism
is the supplanting of politics by law', he strikes a chord with many
recent critics.[22] The two sections to follow unpack this assertion in
detail and show how the policing discourse has grown out of a seeming severance between liberalism and politics, not least through the
rise of legalistic thinking.

## The legacy of legalism

Philosopher Judith Shklar defined 'legalism' as 'the ethical attitude
that holds moral conduct to be a matter of rule following, and moral
relationships to consist of duties and rights determined by rules'.[23]
In the preface of her *Law, Morals and Political Trials* (1986) Shklar
recounts the strength of reaction that the first edition of her book
provoked from the American legal establishment.[24] The chief culprit
for the lawyers enraged by her work, Shklar suggests, is her use of the
term 'ideology'. Shklar uses the term 'ideological' in two senses: to
refer to the 'ideology internal to the legal profession as a social whole'
and a more political sense where 'legalism is projected into the greater
political environment of multiple and competing ideologies', in other

words, not restricted to lawyers.[25] Both senses invoke the idea that a strong faith in the rule of law can be ideological – an understanding that is deeply provocative to those who wish to hold the law 'above' politics.

The point about legalism and part of the explanation for its resonance among liberal thinkers is precisely that it claims to separate law from politics. Whereas politics is generally taken to be a realm of dispute, it is claimed that law represents impartiality and is thus beyond contestation. As Shklar explains, legalists are those who view politics as 'not only something apart from the law, but as inferior to law. Law aims at justice while politics looks only at expediency. The former is neutral and objective, the latter the uncontrolled child of competing interests and ideologies.'[26] Culturally self-conscious, the West had to search for a unique identity in tradition, Shklar argued already in 1964. The core of that tradition is legalism, or the rule of law institutionalised as a policy of justice.[27] In this vein, legal philosopher Ronald Dworkin finds America to be 'obsessed with the law'.[28] This is exactly what Max Weber had in mind when he studied 'rationality': Weber marked out 'the predisposition to discover, construct, and follow rules' as the distinguishing mark of European culture.[29] The Weberian identification of instrumental rationality with Western identity thus mirrors the identification of the tradition of legalism with Western thought.

The separation of law and politics was one of the things most deplored by philosopher Carl Schmitt, staunch critic of the Weimar Republic and notoriously favourably disposed toward the rise of Nazism in Germany in the 1930s.[30] As Heiner Bielefelt points out, Schmitt saw the rule of law as a liberal illusion, both a misconception and hypocrisy.[31] Politics, in Schmitt's view, has only one distinguishing trait: the distinction between friend and enemy – an irreducible distinction, much like that of good and evil in ethics or beautiful and ugly in aesthetics.[32] Schmitt's criticism of liberal legalism has much in common with the realist interpretation of international relations: to the realist, international politics is always about power and interests – and never about morality or law. To link the two, as the first true liberal internationalist, Woodrow Wilson, did, is an offence to the realist mind and Wilson was reviled for it.[33] For Schmitt the triumph of politics over law was most graphically evident under the conditions of emergency, when the rule of law is suspended and sovereign political power resumed. 'Sovereign is he who decides on the state of exception,' Schmitt stated in the opening to his *Political Theology: Four Chapters on the Concept of Sovereignty* (2005 [first published 1922]), by which he meant that a sovereign leader possessed the capacity to make political decisions in the only true sense of the word, that is, 'uncontaminated' by the law.[34]

There are several reasons for the resurgence in interest in the work of Carl Schmitt in recent years. One is clearly frustration with the 'liberal consensus' that has existed since the end of the Cold War, a consensus foundational to the metaphor of war as policing. The way in which the prolonged interventions in Iraq and Afghanistan, not the original invasions, were rationalised was in their ostensible capacity of being 'order-creating': purported to be about the (re) establishment of a rule of law, both internally in respective countries and in relation to a rule-governed global whole. This is the reason that it has been possible to achieve such comparatively broad consensus on the international military presence in Afghanistan and Iraq in spite of massive public resistance at the outset, especially in the case of Iraq. International forces in both contexts have long enjoyed international 'legal' recognition in the form of mandates by the United Nations Security Council. UN Security Council Resolution 1386, which authorised the establishment of the ISAF force to Afghanistan in 2001, and UN SC Resolution 1546 of 2004 that authorised the continued presence of the multinational forces in Iraq thus essentially made it possible for individual states to support the military intervention, however hostile they might have been prior to respective invasion – *with a clear legalist conscience*. The intervention in Iraq is most remarkable in this respect: while the invasion was widely found to contravene international law, Resolution 1546 (2004) effectively shifted the legal grounds from that of 'occupation' to 'support of the new Iraqi government', making continued presence and indeed war-fighting perfectly 'legal'. The great portion (considered in number of years) of the wars in Afghanistan and Iraq has thus taken place with international recognition, and thus not, for that reason at least, violated liberal legalist sensibilities.

The frustration with a liberal consensus in the form of an international system that allows for such radical turn-around as was possible over the invasion of Iraq strikes a chord with those who invoke Schmittian analyses of contemporary international relations – most notably his claim that liberalism papers over differences essential to political life. In Schmitt's words, 'liberals either forget or conceal this political truth – that true differences of opinion in fact do exist'.[35] Much of the unhappiness that exists with the current way of rationalising and understanding war is precisely this: to those concerned with the killing of innocent Iraqi and Afghan civilians by international forces, the fact that such events go unpunished makes a mockery of an international system based on liberal values and the rule of law. Similarly, the ambition of 'restoring' the rule of law (domestically and internationally) by first breaking it appears hypocritical. Moreover, to do so in the technical-managerial way that characterises Western attitudes to military intervention prioritises a simplistic notion of 'fixability' over politics and responsibility.

It may seem odd or counter-intuitive to have the international forces are identified here in terms of their attachment to legalism in war. Much attention has rightly been brought to bear on the *extralegal* aspects of the war on terror. From the abuses committed at the Abu Ghraib prison in Iraq, to the status of prisoners at Guantánamo prison, extraordinary renditions and the use of torture, to the curbing of civil liberties in the name of counterterrorism, inexcusable crimes have been committed in recent years, including by the United States. The Chilcott inquiry in the UK and the ongoing debates in the United States about Guantánamo provide only further evidence of the extent to which Western states squandered legal principles that they had spent such a considerable part of the last half-century attempting to extend to the international realm. Even by defenders liberal advocates, this is criticised: 'we must remain true to our own moral principles', Christopher Coker tells us, 'not because they are universally true but because they are true for us. We must not be seen to be hypocrites, preaching one thing and practising another.'[36] The bottom line of Coker's argument here is a pragmatist one: that these first principles have been developed and relied upon *because they work*: '[Ethics] speaks the language it does not because it approximates to the will of God or the nature of man, but because in the past it was tried, tested and vindicated.'[37]

A second reason for the popularity of Schmittian analysis is found just here, in this recent violation of liberal principles, international law and norms, and the politics of 'exceptionalism' it has generated.[38] To some, the use of torture, extraordinary renditions, Guantánamo and other illegal practices indicate that when the war on terror was declared, the United States assumed the role of the sovereign in the Schmittian sense of being 'he who decides on the exception'. Giorgio Agamben in his *State of Exception* (2005) articulated this view most influentially, and his work has since generated many followers. In this reading, the war on terror instantiated a permanent 'state of exception' on the international level where law is dispensed with and the only politics that exist are the Schmittian kind of 'friend and enemy'.[39]

The point I wish to make here about the relationship between legalism and the contemporary discourse on war is neither to say that the law is always revered by liberals, nor that the war on terror entailed the end of the rule of law on the international level. Clearly, laws have been broken both *in bello* and *ad bellum*, and on occasion conceptions of a rule-governed governed international order have differed between the United States and its allies.[40] To the vast majority of local populations in Afghanistan and Iraq, the liberal world remains unconvincing in its understanding of war. And the supposed 'global liberal consensus', cherished not only by leading liberal democracies but by the international community broadly conceived to include the UN, NGOs and even private security companies in the proclaimed business of 'peacebuilding', seems to do just what Schmitt accused liberals and liberal thought of doing: papering over important differences.

## The problem of politics

To say is that liberalism is no longer political is a popular charge in current debates. The main charges levered against contemporary liberalism by its critics are that it is reductionist, instrumentalist and denies 'the autonomy of the political'.[41] These three assertions are interlinked: liberal political thought is found by many of its critics to be too narrow in its scope and thus reductionist. Moreover, it is found to be instrumentalist, offering only a pre-given list of *wants*, 'prior to the activity of politics'.[42] Finally, critics, especially those drawing on Carl Schmitt, find that liberal thought denies what is essentially political about politics by denying the existence of conflict.

Hardt and Negri's *Empire* spawned debate about liberalism and its global relations. For Hardt and Negri, liberalism *is* empire – not by design, as in the sense that Michael Ignatieff refers to when he talks of 'empire lite' – but inherently so.[43] Hardt and Negri see liberalism in the late twentieth century as dissolving into little more than an extension of capitalism and governmentality on a global scale. Yet there is indeed a global liberal project, whereby liberal elites in the West and in top positions within international institutions such as the UN assume all people around the world want to join.[44] To those who are sceptical of the notion of 'bringing democracy to Iraq' or Afghanistan through military interventions, Todorov's assertion that liberal democracy is a goal universally aspired to ('cherished and desired' by everyone) is not altogether satsifying.

The attempt to cast war as an order-creating enterprise has invited the inextricable conjoining of war with the liberal project as a whole, under the jargon of 'peacebuilding', 'security sector reform', 'local ownership' or 'good governance'. Indeed, this is what we have seen occur since the mid-1990s and that intermingling has been taken to its apotheosis in Afghanistan. Ultimately the contemporary debates around liberalism help explain the conflation of war and state-building (Chapter 3) or conceptions of counterinsurgency as akin to 'peacebuilding' (Chapter 4). Chapter 1 suggested how the narratives invoked in 'conflict analysis' during the 1990s amounted essentially to depoliticised understandings of war. The view of conflict as disorder, the collapse of politics and political life, the letting loose of primordialist hatred in anarchical struggles of all against all were shown to be theories that attempted to 'explain away' conflict as opposed to actually explaining it. From the narratives of non-Western war as essentially constituting descents into 'disorder', a parallel story emerged of conflict management or resolution as the recreation of order through external intervention, including military intervention. This constitutes an integral part of the metaphorical understanding of war as policing that has shaped interventions in Afghanistan and Iraq, as international forces have become deeply embroiled in local insurgencies they helped create in the first place.

As Paul Kelly ponders the future direction of liberalism, he notes two questions relevant for our purposes. First, 'if liberal values are connected with the state and the state is going through a profound process of transformation, what implications does this have for the concerns of liberalism?'[45] Second, 'if liberalism as a political theory being replaced by cosmopolitanism, which is the endorsement of liberal values outside any connection to the institutional structures of the state?'[46] Both these questions strike at the heart of contemporary liberalism as it underpins the policing narrative of war. On the one hand, the prevailing tendency within liberal discourse is to promote cosmopolitan values and thereby also to uphold them by 'policing efforts' around the world.[47] The most conspicuous expression this ambition takes is clearly the attempt to square the upholding of cosmopolitan values and ideals with actual war-fighting – an activity that, despite decision makers' best efforts to change it into something 'less' or more benign than war, remains precisely that.

On the other hand, as I have sought to demonstrate, a discourse on war that imagines war metaphorically as policing is replete with contradictions and tensions – tensions that derive both from within liberalism itself and from changes in more fundamental aspects of our collective consciousness. The existence of such tensions in the models and imaginaries by which the postmodern world interprets itself helps to explain why the metaphorical understanding of war as policing, though widely held, fails to be convincing in practice. As we saw in previous chapters, ambivalence about the role of the state is central both to that collective consciousness (how we imagine political space and the use of political power) and to how the paradox of 'war' and 'policing' is negotiated. To this we must add consideration for collective conceptualisations of agency – a theme of classic concern within liberal thought, but one that has seen significant changes in recent decades.

## Conceptions of agency

Whereas early modern thinkers greatly emphasised the potency of human agency, both individual and collective, 'postmodern liberals' no longer seem to share the Enlightenment faith in human beings' monumental capacity to will and effect change. Faith in the potential of human agency in the postmodern consciousness, in other words, is radically diminished, along with the diminished faith in the capacity of ideology as such. According to theorists of risk such as Beck, Bauman or Giddens, the hyper-modernised world began to lose control over the linear connection between will–action–effect and thereby also its own sense of agency somewhere around the time of the development of the nuclear bomb. At this point Western scientific advancement, the pride of its enlightened capacity for scientific thinking, had outdone itself. It had produced consequences over which it no longer had control. What was previously thought of as unobjectionably good – scientific advancement – no longer appeared to be good or even useful. From the nuclear bomb to the disaster of global warming, insecurity over genetically modified crops and other foods or anything else, technological advancement today generates anxiety and fear, as risk theorists tell us. Along with this, human agency itself needs to be reconceptualised, sociologists tell us, with 'reflexivity' cast as the operative term.[48]

Anxiety over the future consequences of present-day action is the very opposite of a positive description of agency. Reflexive rationality and the scramble to mitigate future potential consequences of current action thus seem to signal a radically different conception of agency from that of classical modernity. The legalist legacy of liberalism only further diminishes the ideal or sense of agency in that it readily conjures up a programmatic interpretation of the liberal values it was designed to protect and advance. The modern Weberian understanding of rationality as inherently instrumental has indeed been dealt a blow, in part by the gradual rise in reflexive reasoning, yet it is by no means gone. There is an immense amount of attachment also among liberals today to the notion that we act instrumentally. What makes the conceptualisation of agency complex and contradictory is that there *is* indeed still a will to effect change by human action, and the liberal international project is the most dominant expression thereof. Yet, as we have seen, it is a watered-down, minimalist project – it no longer carries the same force among its protagonists as it did in the classic modern period. This has enabled the current technocratic slant on liberal internationalism: the strict focus on 'capacity-building', programmatic 'security sector reform', and so on.

The force of the liberal project has changed in part due to more fundamental changes in the way the world is perceived, including the reshaping of social and political relations across the globe arising from globalisation and the ushering in of supraterritorial, instantaneous hyperconnectivity. The emphasis on the individual that the modern period stood for has morphed into an atomisation of individuals and an adjacent decline in both individual and collective sense of agency. David Chandler is among those who have pointed to 'a more atomised politics of self-expression – of awareness, of identity and values'.[49] In other words, values still do play an important role in the way we understand the world, our role in it, and ultimately war.

It follows from this that the sometime juxtaposition of Western war as 'instrumental' against the 'expressive' or 'existentialist' warfare of others is utterly deceptive. War is neither instrumental nor existential war: it is both. War is always to some extent involves imparting meaning to actions, as anthropologists tell us.[50] Usually cast as an issue of 'culture', the meanings we impart to events and actions vary: to recognise that human beings are 'historical and culture-bearing social beings engaged in relations of meaning-creation and symbolism' does not, as critics may want to assert, amount to a cultural-relativist positions, but simply that we ought be mindful of the context in which something occurs and the specific *communicative* meaning it carries in that specific context.[51] This is as much the case for troops from the international coalitions in Iraq or Afghanistan as for the individual who blows himself up in the hope of sending a message. The weak postmodern account of agency does not invite recognition that what each and every one of us does matters, not least in war, which is now almost exclusively determined at the tactical rather than the strategic level. In other words, we tend to be oblivious to the consequences individual action carries, in part because it resonates with the postheroic understanding of war in the contemporary West.[52]

If the real legacy of modernity is the global reach of nihilism, in Gray's words, this would seem to constitute another testimony to the diminished role of individual/collective agency in the postmodern collective consciousness.[53] Gray draws on the Nietzschean prediction that the ultimate destiny of the Enlightenment project was to find that the capacity for instrumental reason would eventually be reduced to a 'will to power'.[54] The result of this Nietzschean prediction is the abandonment of all moral principles coupled with the view that life is meaningless. Thus, 'nothing remains of this [the Enlightenment] project but the expansion of human productive powers through technological domination of the earth'; and it is precisely this will that is now being spread globally.[55] In other words, the result of the Western humanist project is the will to power, maintaining struggle with everyone else.

## Resistance

We do all of this today against an enemy unrecognisable from the past, indeed unprecedented. It is the completely unconstrained terrorist. We face an adversary which revels in mass murder; which sets out to cause the greatest pain it can to innocent people; which is entirely unconstrained by any law; which sees all civilians, including women and children not as non-combatants but as easy targets; which sees terror as a key part of its arsenal, and which both glorifies and operates suicide bombers. It is an enemy, unfettered by any sense of morality – indeed it is spurred on by a perverse perception of morality to achieve ever-greater extent of civilian carnage. ... *Where we intrinsically value life, they do not.*[56]

This statement by then UK Defence Secretary John Reid from 2006 poignantly reveals the desire to describe the enemy in Iraq and Afghanistan (and elsewhere) as utterly estranged from 'reason'. Western policymakers, especially in the years immediately following 9/11, have been keen to describe insurgents in Iraq and Afghanistan as having an apocalyptic will towards destruction, ultimately portraying them as less than human. We are thus seeing spokesmen for leading liberal states identifying others as nihilists: thus, the most readily accessible explanation for militant Islam to John Reid seemed to be that these people were 'unfettered by any sense of morality' and do not 'intrinsically value life'.[57] That this was a convenient way of 'explaining' militant Islamism, and the opposition the international forces came to face in Iraq and Afghanistan is not surprising. After all, it fit exceptionally well with narratives that preceded the preoccupation with terrorism: it followed the same basic line of argument that non-Western warring in essence constituted simply a breakdown of order as we saw emerge in the 1990s. These narratives were given a new spin and tremendous new force under the war on terror.

Crucially, the policing discourse fails to convince or compel its intended subjects. The very categories set up to distinguish 'legitimate' from 'illegitimate' actors in war – the lists of proscribed 'terrorist organisations', whether under the aegis of individual states such as the US or the UK, or international organisations such as the EU or the UN – quite obviously do not command universal support and are clearly refuted by the individuals and organisations listed. The opponents of the international forces in Iraq or Afghanistan do not likely see themselves as 'thugs or criminals' with a general ambition only to wreck havoc and disorder – nor do they see intervening forces as having the ambition of 'restoring order'.[58] And nor do they, as Todorov optimistically claims, see liberal democracy as 'a model that is cherished and desired everywhere'.[59]

On account of the global ambitions of other fighters, Olivier Roy in *Globalized Islam: The Search for a New Ummah* (2002) places the rise of global jihadism in the context of globalisation itself. Roy thus seeks the social conditions under which jihadist action takes place in the structure of global relations.[60] In this account, the new community of global jihadists is one that transcends geography (in this sense it chimes well with Jan Aart Scholte's notion of supraterritoriality). Moreover, there are important affinities between Olivier Roy's analysis and that offered by John Gray in *Al Qaeda and What it Means to be Modern* (2003): both see the rise of al-Q'aeda and global jihadism more broadly as distinctly *modern* phenomena. For Roy, 'Islamic revivalism goes hand in hand' with the 'culture of the self' – a preoccupation of the classic modernist creed.[61] Such aspirations do not produce subjects who are readily 'policed' in the context of war.

While much attention in 2010–11 focused on the US surge in troop numbers and US General Stanley McChrystal's appropriation of 'state of the art' counterinsurgency strategy, the fact that negotiations were eventually pursued with the Taliban garnered less attention than one might have expected.[62] Also, a statement by the United Nations Assistance Mission to Afghanistan (UNAMA) in March 2010 indicated that the UN was from there on to officially take part in 'consultations' with Hezb-e-Islami, an insurgent group associated with the Taliban.[63] Support for potential negotiations constitutes a veritable sea change from the previous 'capture or kill' policy of the international forces. Given that the US-led troops had as their immediate objective the removal of the Taliban from power in 2001, one cannot but raise an eyebrow at the irony of this outcome.

## Liberal internationalism and the discriminating concept of war

When Chris Patten, British high-profile politician, was accused by a right-wing American commentator in the early days of the George W. Bush administration of being a 'liberal internationalist', his reply was to state that: 'To my mind there is nothing else for a sensible person to be.'[64] Patten's reply points to the pervasiveness of liberal internationalism in early twenty-first-century debates on international security: from Tony Blair's 1999 Chicago speech a couple of weeks into the Kosovo War, when he famously declared 'we are all internationalists now', the language and practice of liberal internationalism has become a direction in international politics that is much taken for granted. The advent of the war on terror did, of course, represent something of a break by bringing into relief the potency of the United States to flaunt international opinion: before the March 2003 the world may have been cognisant of America's 'unipolar moment', just what it might entail when put to the test was unknown.[65] Most significantly the declaration of a war on terror by Bush in 2001 changed international affairs by altering the terms of debate on issues such as the (until then) popular notion of 'humanitarian intervention' and 'responsibility to protect'.[66] Yet, for all these changes, on balance, and with Bush's retreat from the international scene, it seems that less changed in terms of the liberal internationalist agenda itself than what was perhaps thought at the outset of the war on terror.

The motivation offered by *Prospect Magazine* for the nomination of General David Petraeus as 'public intellectual of the year' was that his doctrine constituted 'the first actively humane war fighting doctrine ever to come out of the Pentagon, enshrining the ideas that winning a modern war requires ensuring the security and wellbeing of the civilian population, that humanitarian assistance and construction projects are critical to any fight'.[67] The point is less that *Prospect* editors thought the Petraeus doctrine 'intellectual'; what is interesting is rather that it is conceived as the *only possible* intellectual approach to war-fighting. This is testimony to how widespread and pervasive the metaphorical understanding of military intervention in a foreign country as an order-restorative force has become. The concept of security has been discussed to a phenomenal degree in the last two decades, from the fall of the Berlin Wall and the collapse of the Soviet Union to the ticking on of the wars in Iraq and Afghanistan, and the extension of the war on terror to Somalia, Yemen, the Niger Delta and so on. From a 'widened' security concept, via human security to the securitisation debate and lastly the claims about global governmentality and a permanent state of exception, we recognise the conflating of liberal discourses from a range of fields with the enterprise of military engagement. The metaphor of war as policing thus amounts to a discourse that encompasses the many varieties of jargonised language of 'peacebuilding', 'counterinsurgency', 'local ownership' and so on.

The distinction made by Philip Windsor between 'values' and 'norms' – seeing values as being translated into norms of social behaviour – is illuminating with respect to what appears to have gone awry for the liberal internationalist project.[68] Indeed it is the instrumentalisation of liberal values through war-fighting that demands interrogation; and liberal values have been put to some rather extreme instrumentalisation in the interventions in Afghanistan and Iraq. Liberal internationalism is put to practice through various agents – including the UN and regional organisations, global financial institutions, and individual states – but never is the instrumentalisation of liberal values as crude as when it takes the form of war-fighting. Yet the point of the metaphorical imagination of war as order-creating, directed against enemies conceived as 'criminal' or 'terrorist' is precisely that it evades discussion of war itself: it purports to make 'war' less warlike.

This is precisely what Carl Schmitt identified as liberalism's 'discriminating concept of war'.[69] Writing between 1937 and 1945, Schmitt's critique was directed against the League of Nations and the international system of jurisprudence that was developed for its insistence on the existence of universal standards of 'humanity'. To Schmitt, the treaty of Versailles and the League of Nations system then established revolutionalised the concept of war by transforming it into a *discriminating* concept, based on the League's self-declared right to decide what party was to be considered 'just' in a conflict, and the authority to declare this decision binding on all other parties.[70] For Schmitt, it is the aspiration to universality encompassed in the discriminating concept of war that is most problematic: it assumes that one side can uncontroversially be declared 'right', and that therefore war against its opponents simply is not 'war' proper. 'The Geneva League of Nations', Schmitt wrote, 'if it is anything appreciable at all, is fundamentally a system of legalization, a system that monopolizes judgement on the just war.'[71] Presciently, he pointed to the interest in a discriminating concept of war on the part of the victorious powers of England, France and the US, whereby those deemed in the wrong would no longer be regarded as 'warring parties' but their war-fighting seen rather as an 'international crime' and therefore a 'policeable action'.[72] What Schmitt saw in the juris-prudence of Versailles and Nuremburg was the introduction of an authoritative policy of discrimination that fundamentally questioned not only the non-discriminating concept of war, but indeed *any* concept of war. 'In reality, the question is no longer: just war or unjust war, allowed or forbidden war. Rather, it becomes: war or no war?'[73]

The critique Schmitt levered in the interwar period as regards lib-eralism's universalising tendency, potential and aspirations is highly poignant as regards the liberal imagination of war 'as' policing. Ushered in by the combination of an international system where sanction by the United Nations Security Council makes the use of military force something 'other' than war, and a liberal international-ist wave that has so decisively conjoined the use of force with a 'post-ideological' politics of the global promotion of liberal democracy, neoliberal economic policy and a humanitarian creed, the policing narrative represents the present-day version of a regime that has effected precisely a discriminating concept of war. In practical terms, just as Schmitt predicted, this means: 'war and yet no war at the same time; anarchy; and chaos in international law' (hence the 'nor-malisation of war' described in Chapter 2).[74] Boutros-Boutros Ghali's words from 1992 echo: at this point, he claimed, the world stood a unique chance of creating a 'new world order'.[75] That this ambition would team up with the 'unending war' of promoting a 'security-development' nexus and result in a resurgence of a new discrimi-nating concept of war under the metaphor of policing to combat 'disorderly' elements to the extent seen with the massive interven-tions in Afghanistan and Iraq was perhaps hard to imagine.[76] Yet the formidable dominance of liberalism in the post-Cold War era – combined with the emergence of an adjacent, very particular, view of the opponents of such 'liberal internationalism' – illustrates the readiness with which the policing narrative was absorbed in the first decade of the twenty-first century. It fit, in other words, with broader tendencies: with contemporary Western social imaginaries and the intellectual scaffolding of dominant liberal political thought.

### 'Absent enemies': politics without conflict and war without antagonism

What accounts for the assumption that others will want what liberal leaders want them to want? Chantal Mouffe's potent critique of the description of the present era as 'post-ideological' or 'post-political' focuses on the absence of *conflict* in such descriptions of the realm of the political.[77] Touched upon in the discussion of the relationship between political space/spatiality, conceptions of politics and conceptions of war in Chapter 3, the dominance of accounts of contemporary politics, both global and local, as having outlived traditional ideological divides is striking in contemporary debates. Work by sociologists like Anthony Giddens, Ulrich Beck and Zygmunt Bauman has been tremendously influential in terms of ushering in discussions of a new type of politics, focused not on *political* difference but played out in the realm of morality, where the old 'left and right' has made way for 'right and wrong'. As Mouffe points out, such descriptions utterly efface the antagonistic dimension of the political.[78] Imagining a world 'beyond' sovereignty, 'beyond' antagonism, 'beyond' left and right fit perfectly with the imagination of the possibility of a 'new world order' emerging – where the opponents of that world order were cast in terms of being simply 'wrong' – symptomatic of 'disorder', 'criminality' or 'terrorism'.

The policing narrative on war is the vision of the 'post-political' writ large: the rendering invisible of opposition to liberal internationalist visions. In this narrative, opposition to liberal internationalist ideals becomes mere 'technical' issues of 'implementation', prompting the incessant scramble for new ways of 'perfecting' the practice of 'post-conflict reconstruction', 'peacebuilding', 'counterinsurgency' or 'counterterrorism'. As Mouffe points out, liberal theorists refuse to acknowledge the antagonistic dimension of politics – the existence of real opposition – because to do so would endanger the pretences of consensus, a 'consensus' available through use of reason (which in turn liberals see as the aim of democracy).[79] *Enemies* are thus absent: this is a politics 'without frontiers, without a "they" – a win-win politics in which solutions could be found favouring everybody in society'.[80] Through the liberal internationalist creed, the vision of the 'post-political' has been transposed to the international realm, and with it a 'post-adversarial' understanding of war.

Given that they assume 'consensus', policing wars embody a set of assumptions both about the 'insurgent' opponents they face, as well as about the local populations and the way in which they can be 'known' in the context of war. Informed by the notion of 'winning hearts and minds', policing wars in their most recent counterinsurgency guise are guided by a logic that assumes that political *opposition* can with certainty be overcome: that the people 'among' whom war is fought can be made to support the mission of the intervening forces, that their hearts and minds can, in fact, be won.[81] Unsurprisingly then, COIN FM 3–24 refers to 'governance' 45 times and 'legitimacy' 88 times, and memorably invokes the idea of 'armed social work'; in COIN logic, war is 'civilianised' through and through.[82] Marginalised from counterinsurgency thinking, then, is *antagonism*: policing war in its COIN guise is about *persuasion*, a task that demands engagement with all levels and aspects of societal life, from social and economic development to political and administrative structures to psychological dimensions. It is, in short, a politics of life in life's totality.

The recent turn in counterinsurgency thinking toward a focus on communication, and in particular the notion of 'strategic communication', is particularly noteworthy as regards what it tells us about the conception of enemies in a 'post-political' vision of conflict and war. 'Strategic communication' (SC) was identified in the 2006 US *Quadrennial Defense Review* (QDR) as being one of five areas of particular emphasis, and further highlighted by President Obama in 2009 as a centrepiece of the new 'AfPak' strategy.[83] Also in 2009 Obama instructed the creation of a new unit within the State Department dedicated to SC and declared $150 million (£92 million) made available yearly for 'strategic communication' in Afghanistan and Pakistan.[84] SC takes the logic of policing wars to its extreme by positing that if only local populations would receive the 'right message' about what the intervening forces are attempting to do in Afghanistan/Pakistan, they can be made to support the mission. The problem of 'insurgency' is thus reduced to being of two kinds: either those *not yet* persuaded but possible to persuade through effective communication strategies, or not *possible* to persuade.[85] The *Joint Forces Commander's Handbook on Strategic Communication and Communication Strategy* of 2010 thus advocates compiling biographical data, including 'character trait data' on 'leaders' core beliefs and values, 'perceptual biases' and decision-making styles, for psychological profiling use to identify the 'appropriate' targeting of different groups – as well as the identification of those groups thought not worth targeting with communication campaigns for they do not share the 'universal' aspirations of all 'reasonable' people: they are 'terrorists'.

This understanding of 'insurgents', of the populations among whom they 'swim' and of these populations' political agency is endemic to contemporary counterinsurgency thinking. As Alan Cromartie demonstrates, FM 3–24 relies on a view of the 'culture' of the populations among whom war takes place as composed of a set of identifiable human 'motivations' and 'beliefs'; a 'culture', it is assumed, which can successfully be 'altered'.[86] Notable practices in this regard have included the deployment of Human Terrain Teams and the use of so-called Culture Smart Cards. The possibility of a genuinely dissenting view, an actual antagonistic position that is genuinely and positively held, is left entirely unpursued. The fundamental assumption of 'strategic communication' as it features in recent counterinsurgency thinking is that any opposition to the message communicated is conceived of as a communication problem, not a problem of genuine difference or dissent. *Enlisting Madison Avenue: The Marketing Approach to Earning Popular Support in Theatres of Operation*, a 2007 RAND study, epitomizes just such thinking, and indeed the study was later to greatly influence US' military thinking on the communications element of counterinsurgency strategy. The outlandish title alone is indicative of the reliance on strategies of persuasion from an entirely different realm – that of commercial and marketing logics – into the realm of warfare.

We can trace in this account of 'absent enemies' a particular view then of human agency. As a key element of any era's intellectual scaffolding, conceptions of agency, and notably political agency, contribute to the sustaining of particular imageries of war (along with conceptions of time, space and power). As we saw earlier, the formidable faith placed in the capacity of human beings to effect *change* was an integral part of early modern political thought. In the contemporary world, teleological thinking, generally ideologically informed and with strong notions of political agency, stands in contrast with a technocratic liberalism that allows for no 'real' political opponents but only temporary 'obstacles'. Yet, for the insistence on the absence of enemies in policing war, resistance still exists, of course. As Mouffe points out, conflict does not go away in the face of the story of the post-political. It is only that the opponents are demonised to an extent that removes them from the realm of 'politics': they demonised as 'terrorists', with whom no political dialogue is possible. This mirrors the designation of radical opponents by the theorists of 'reflexive modernisation' as described by Beck and Giddens – the only opponent such models envisage is that of the 'fundamentalist' who, in reaction to reflexive modernity, attempts to reassert 'traditional' (outdated) values.[87]

None of this is to suggest, of course, that persuasion has entirely taken over from killing in contemporary policing wars: kinetic warfare often in the form of Special Forces' operations and drone attacks, are integral to contemporary counterinsurgency strategy.[88] Rather, it is the *rationalisation* of killing that is altered in counterinsurgency logic. The only antagonistic element acknowledged in this war is towards enemies unrecognised in political terms in one of two ways: either as beyond the realm of politics ('terrorist') or assumed amenable to persuasion. Since President Obama assumed office in 2009, the shift towards the 'other' side of counterinsurgency war – that of a highly kinetic 'shadow war' involving an increasing reliance on Special Forces' secret operations and the advent of large-scale drone warfare – has been perceptible. The shift towards this side of counterinsurgency thinking would seem to indicate the demise of the post-Cold War and post-9–11 rationalisation of war as policing; yet, the extent of this demise remains to be seen as the shadow side of counterinsurgency warfare is beginning to emerge out of the shadows.

## Conclusion

Tying together the understandings of law and politics that underpin the metaphorical view of war as policing, this chapter has explored both the legacy of the liberal tendency towards legalism and the liberal tendency to assume that liberal international politics are, or rightly should be, unchallenged. Above all, the intermingling of the wider liberal project with war-fighting as such has created an irremediable muddle of 'counterinsurgency', 'peacebuilding', 'development' or 'democracy' promotion and so on. Under the dominant discourse of war they are all taken to be part of the same order-creating, policing logic of twenty-first-century intervention.

Yet, to state the obvious, opponents of the international forces in Afghanistan and Iraq do not see themselves as fighting a neutral order-creating force but as defending against an intrusive force that pretends to be universally appreciated, while co-opting their local foes. The insurgents in Afghanistan and Iraq refuse to be effectively *policed*; they evidently have a very different understanding of what these wars are about, and are not about to be convinced by the liberal tale of universalism, humanism and legalism. The fact that liberal states (and liberal elites more broadly) stubbornly refuse to take heed of this discrepancy means both that the liberal world continues to go 'misunderstood' in its quest; and that unrealistic expectations on what war can achieve continue to be fostered.[89] Thus, the logic of counterinsurgency is built on the idea that it is possible to win the 'trust' of local populations – and that there is no contradiction between establishing trust and dropping bombs.

As this final chapter has shown, part of the explanation lies in the notion of political agency that underpins contemporary liberalism. The weak conception of agency inherent in the policing metaphor is indicative of the programmatic and schematic understanding of what war is, and its naively technocratic assumptions about what the use of military force can achieve. A problem with much of the critique of the contemporary approaches to war is that they argue that the ambitions of wars in Iraq and Afghanistan (on the part of the international forces) are not genuine, that the COIN campaigns there mask other motives. This book says differently: the beliefs are deeply and genuinely held. However, they are illusory. They are illusory because they fail to see that the legalism of the understanding of war *is* in fact challenged; and that insurgents in Iraq and Afghanistan are active agents with a will beyond violating efforts at strengthening 'governance' or 'state-building'. Quite obviously, they see themselves as having a purpose beyond the violation of order. The crisis of liberal internationalism is brought about by the failures of the contemporary approach to war – and in turn calls for a re-thinking of the way in which liberalism is instrumentalised militarily on the global level in the twenty-first century.

# Conclusion

## Policing wars

Investigating the preoccupation in the first decade of the twenty-first century with actors depicted as 'criminal' in war – the 'terrorists', 'warlords' and 'insurgents' of this world – was one of the original impetuses for this book. When scholars like Michael Howard or John Mueller asserted that war 'no longer existed', that all that remained was 'criminal activity' that the liberal world had a duty to 'police', in what context were they making those claims? 'Policing' does not make sense on the international level: there is no clear authority – no Leviathan – whose laws can be enacted or policed, yet some general climate of opinion appeared to allow Howard, Mueller and others to invoke the language of policing. Their language was mirrored by leaders who championed the vision of a 'post-political' world, where liberal internationalism was seen as unchallenged, other than by 'fundamentalist' opponents. Throughout this book, it has been argued that the *policing* referred to both in the mainstream academic literature and by key liberal leaders, notably in the US and the UK but also in a wider liberal elite, is a *metaphorical kind of policing* – the imagination of the use of military force not as a coercive, destructive force, but as order-creating, directed against those who create 'disorder', whose action is not deemed 'political' but obstructive of a general 'progression' towards a liberal world order.

At first glance, it seemed that this preoccupation with 'criminal' or 'terrorist' opponents in war was tied exclusively to the war on terror. Without doubt, the attacks on the United States on 11 September 2001 and the subsequent declaration by then President George W. Bush of a 'global war on terror' constituted key events in the opening of the twenty-first century. Perhaps the most common critique (shared by writers on opposite ends of the political spectrum) levered against the Bush administration immediately post-9/11 was that President George W. Bush had made a tremendous mistake in declaring a *war* on the terrorists that had carried out the attacks on New York and Washington, DC that sunny September morning, and that instead he should have declared not only that the attacks were criminal in nature but that they would be persecuted through global juridical mechanisms. What these critics had in mind, however, was not a metaphorical understanding of *war as policing*, but *actual policing*. Their reasoning hinged on the existence of global mechanisms for justice, and the ability of the international community to come together behind their concerted use, in a manner that was globally acceptable.

Of course, things developed differently. Though efforts are being made in the direction of global jurisdiction, such a system is far from reality; and it was easy for the Bush administration to discount that route. Instead, the wars in Afghanistan and Iraq followed. These wars came to be supremely influential in debates far beyond the original frame of a 'war on terror', and outlasted the succession of leaders in both the states that led the interventions in the first place, the United States and the United Kingdom. As we have seen, the invention or emergence of a conceptual metaphor cannot be attributed to a single fact, event or 'cause' in any other sense. Instead, to interrogate the reasons behind a shared reliance on any conceptual metaphor, including the one under scrutiny of war understood metaphorically as policing, we have had to look toward the shared social imaginaries and basic assumptions contained therein. Conceptual or cognitive metaphors migrate into language because they are shared by a *culture*; indeed, the emergence and subsequent sharing of a conceptual metaphor can play a significant part in the very construction of a culture.[1] The processes of culture-construction is constantly ongoing; thus to investigate the reasons behind the emergence and sustaining of a metaphorical understanding of war as policing, we have had to consider also the constitutive parts of a culture. The culture under scrutiny is that of the contemporary liberal world, characterised, *inter alia*, by a postmodern imagination of politics.

Three claims were made in the Introduction about the possible meaning and content of the metaphorical understanding of war as policing in contemporary liberal discourse. First, it was suggested that it implied an understanding of the wars in Afghanistan and Iraq as a necessary 'corrective' to the unlawful behaviour of criminal, terrorist others. We have seen over the course of this book various explanations for how this understanding of war had come to be. As demonstrated in Chapter 1, debate about conflicts (in most cases not involving Western states) prior to 9/11 and the war on terror tended to de-emphasise political causes of conflict. Instead the narratives that had taken hold at the end of the last century largely explained conflict as *disorder*: they stressed a purported unreason on the part of the (non-Western) fighters, and described violence as 'senseless' and 'anarchic'. The view of conflict as breakdown or collapse of the normal order – indeed, the collapse of politics *per se* – coincided with a surge of optimism about the prospects for a new, liberal, international order made possible by the end of the Cold War. Interventions by the international community (both the UN and individual states, such as Britain in Sierra Leone or the United States in Somalia) were conceived as responses to disorder, striving toward a (re)creation of order.

In Chapter 3 we saw how the modern predisposition towards the state as the only legitimate site of politics also had a role in explaining scepticism about conflicts wherein the protagonists did not necessarily make control of the central government their only or central aim. Despite the advent of new spatial structures in the postmodern era, this vision lingers, and insurgents whose aims do not involve seeking control over a state are frequently essentialised as either petty criminals or nihilistic terrorists. And in Chapter 5 we saw how liberalism's legalistic tendencies predisposed liberal observers of contemporary war towards a view of political normality as rule-governed. This liberal heritage thus constitutes an ideal image that invites liberals to take a view of the (non-rule-governed) violence of others as essentially *un*-political.

The second claim made in the Introduction about the possible meaning of the metaphorical understanding of war as policing was about the expectation that we might productively achieve social change in a target society in the context of war. This expectation was found to be the counterpart of the narratives of conflict as 'disorder', analysed in Chapter 1: namely, the response emanating from liberal states and international organisations from the UN to the EU that international responses to conflict should be constituted as *responses to disorder.* We noted also a general unwillingness to think of such interventions as 'war', even if they involved the use of military force in very hostile situations, and a large-scale partnering of military force with civilian elements under banners of 'military–civilian integration', 'state-building', 'security-development nexus', 'military humanitarianism' and so on. Briefly discussed in Chapter 1, this theme was returned to in Chapter 4 on conceptions of power, which discussed the way in which the building of local security forces in the context of war in Afghanistan and Iraq is seen as an effort to transfer power and even 'authority' under recent counterinsurgency strategies.

The third claim about the liberal predisposition towards viewing war metaphorically as policing was that it reflects an assumption that war can not only be used to create order, but indeed a specific type of order, a liberal democratic order, in target states. This was expanded on in Chapters 4 and 5, which both discussed the idealised images of how democratic governance supposedly can be 'established' in the context of war. The translation of such idealised images into little more than a technical checklist of features expected from a democratically governed state, and the attempt to make this checklist materialise in the context of war is a highly tenuous thing. The holding of elections, for example, constitutes one way of channelling such ambitions – an effort that has yielded disappointing results in both Iraq and Afghanistan where elections have been mired in fraud – yet the international community that insisted on the elections in the first place was forced to tacitly let this pass. This point was not lost on the Taliban, which issued an astute statement on 3 November 2009, after a second round of elections in Afghanistan was cancelled:

> The cancellation of the second round of the election showed that decisions on Afghanistan are made in Washington and London, while the announcements are made in Kabul. ... What is astonishing is two weeks ago they were arguing that the puppet president Hamid Karzai was involved in electoral fraud ... but now he is elected as president based on those same fraudulent votes, Washington and London immediately send their congratulations.[2]

All three assertions about the metaphorical imagination of war as policing are manifest in the debate about 'counterinsurgency' (as was discussed in detail in Chapter 4). As Paul Cornish has argued, the idea 'that there must be one strategic paradigm – one style of war-fighting – which outranks all others and which should become the exclusive focus of defence planners, doctrine specialists, military trainers, and so on' has been particularly potent since the end of the Cold War.[3] Since the Petraeus 'surge' in Iraq, later transposed to Afghanistan, the strategic paradigm was 'COIN'. Yet, as the discussion in Chapter 4 demonstrated, counterinsurgency is but the most recent reincarnation of the policing metaphor, sharing many of the attributes of other 'order-creating' narratives of the past decades, notably the narratives of 'peacebuilding' and the promotion of 'good governance'. The shared assumption underpinning them all is that domestic order can productively be *created* in a target state through external intervention – and that this task includes the establishment of physical security, a new purported rule of law, political representation, protection of civil liberties, minority rights and so on.

To summarise the discourse on war in the early twenty-first century, it consists of three, in the liberal world, deeply held sets of beliefs. First, the preconceived view among liberal decision-makers that 'policing', metaphorically understood, will work. This is the essence of the view that non-Western war-fighting is 'disorderly', and that liberal states and organisations can intervene, also militarily, to recreate order. Second, we have the idealistic view, inspired by moral and ethical claims, that 'policing' *should* work. This view is informed by a host of preconceptions about politics, law and war that were discussed in Chapter 5. Third, we have the value statement that policing *ought* to work. This is the liberal predisposition towards a legalistic view of politics transposed into war – albeit a liberalism less certain about its foundations and less messianic than in the early modern period. As Timothy Nunan points out in his introduction to the recently translated collection of Carl Schmitt's writings on war, in seeking to understand how a given international system works, 'you must ask how a war is defined, as well as who decides when something is called war'.[4] In Chapter 5 we saw how the Schmittian critique of liberalism, directed against the system of jurisprudence established with the Versailles Treaty in 1919, continues to hold formidable sway in the twenty-first century when liberal leaders anew conceive the term 'war' in a discriminatory fashion.

By unpacking the various origins of the policing metaphor for war and the fundamental 'intellectual scaffolding' on which it rests,

I have throughout this book identified tensions and contradictions inherent in the policing metaphor. Put into practice, this discourse on war results in wars that appear interminable in any decisive way, as we saw in Chapter 2 on time and temporality. These wars are ill-contained also in spatial terms, as Chapter 3 demonstrated. The effort to 'transfer' power and even authority from intervening forces to newly created local ones, described in Chapter 4, is contradictory and posits goal ultimately impossible to achieve. The bottom line here is that it is not possible to *will* something on behalf of another, as in *willing* Afghan or Iraqi citizens to seek democratic governance.

Finally, we have an inherent tension in the conception of political agency that seems to underpin much of the contemporary liberal imagination. In the modern era, liberals were keenly aware that those of other political persuasions (fascist or communist) had as strong a sense of *their* agency as liberals did of their own. People's tremendous belief in the potential of human agency ultimately translated into total war, where annihilation of the enemy was the final objective. In the contemporary era, we see a different type of tension in the liberal imagination of agency: agency on the part of liberal actors in war is *assumed*, albeit not with the same fervent conviction as previously, but the agency of opponents in war is ignored or obliterated altogether. Opponents of the international forces in Iraq and Afghanistan over the course of the wars in the respective location have generally been considered as either too banal to be political (petty or disorderly criminals) or too nihilistic to be considered political opponents (the jihadists). The metaphorical understanding of war as 'policing', essentially promoting a universally shared aspiration towards rule-bound conceptions of order, does not seem to have compelled the local populations in Iraq and Afghanistan, and even less the insurgents fighting what they see as an illegitimate presence of foreign troops. The recent turn in counterinsurgency strategy towards a focus on 'strategic communication' exposes the insistence on the absence of 'real' enemies – opponents who have a political ground for resistance – in favour of the demonisation of 'die hard' terrorists. All others, in counterinsurgency thinking, can be 'persuaded' – thus is the logic of 'post-adversarial' politics writ global and enacted through the use of military force.

Yet, the discourse on war war metaphorically as policing has been remarkably resilient. Interestingly, failures of the discourse to translate into results in reality have consistently been attributed to a *failure of implementation*, rather than the failure of the actual ideas that sustain this imagination of war. The focus on 'failures of implementation' has recurred in debates about counterinsurgency, of the British 'comprehensive approach' or of 'peacebuilding' alike. Indeed, as regards any incarnation of the policing metaphor, the stubborn conclusion appears to be that it has simply not been done well enough. If only it was done perfectly, if the most sophisticated minds were put to work in articulating every detail of the perfect counterinsurgency mindset, and these principles were then duly acted upon by all from the top leadership to the individual soldier, the results desired would materialise – thus insist the protagonists of a liberal internationalism based a discriminating concept of war.

The metaphorical understanding of war as policing is an idea held by a global liberal elite, found in the West as well as in many parts of the international community of liberal opinion. Indeed, it is a constitutive part of that culture, and the metaphorical understanding of war as policing has crept into a shared liberal, technocratic vernacular, as cognitive metaphors tend to do. It is not an understanding universally shared. The opponents of the international forces in Iraq, Afghanistan, Pakistan, Somalia, Yemen, Colombia or elsewhere do not see themselves as resisting a legitimate 'policing' force, as a criminal or delinquent would in the domestic context. Criminals *knowingly* break the law; they do not generally challenge the *existence* or righteousness of law in the first place. This constitutes a significant difference to the actual wars that are being fought under the current discourse, and this is the reason that I have shown the discourse to be informed by a *metaphor* of policing: it has not *become* policing. 'Policing' is nonsensical if there is no agreed authority, which, on the global level, there is not; yet decision-makers continue to insist that the failures of war constitute failures of implementation, imperfections of the *means* of war, not of war's aims or ends. Recall Charles Taylor's words quoted in Chapter 2 that for the postmodern world 'everything had become a matter of means' and nothing is any longer 'a matter of ends'. This is the epitome of the policing metaphor.

The possibility that the intellectual scaffolding of our time, the conceptual structures that allow us to make sense of social and political life and its development, is undergoing radical change in the transition from modernity to postmodernity is one that has been seriously entertained in this book. In other words, it is not to the matter of 'failure' to correctly implement the ideas and idealisations of war but a fundamental rupture of ideas themselves – the mental structures on which we build our sense of self and sense of meaning – that we ought to look if we are to understand the crisis of political thinking as it relates to, and plays out, thinking on war.

## The intellectual scaffolding of twenty-first-century liberalism

What then have we learnt about the possible 'intellectual scaffolding' of liberal thought in the early twenty-first century? Over the course of this book, several structuring ideas have been contemplated. In Chapter 2, we saw how the transition from modern to postmodern conditions entailed a relinquishing of linear conceptions of time and temporality – not in a metaphysical sense but time in the sense of *durée* and historicity: the way in which any society (or individual) conceptualises its place in history. Under postmodern conditions, we seem 'trapped' in a radical present – a present that needs constantly to be legitimated on its own terms. No longer is it possible to defend present-day actions as means towards an end, present-day actions can no longer be legitimated instrumentally in terms of a better future. Instead, present actions must be able to stand on their own, to be legitimated on their own terms. In part this is a comforting thought – it seems to ward off the excesses of the modern period, where the present was squeezed into insignificance in the name of a utopian future. Yet, living in a radical or endless present is also destabilising for it means that we lose sight of the purpose of actions. This consequence is clearly reflected in current wars, where the question of *how* the liberal world fights is raised more often than the question of *why* or *for what purpose*.

Conceptualisations of political space and spatiality are also affected in the transition from modernity to postmodernity. The immediate and powerful identification of politics with the territorial state in the modern period is increasingly being challenged by non-territorial forms of political association – notably through the prominence of networks and instantaneous, supraterritorial connections. These changes as to the way that political spatiality is imagined has led to certain conflicts being considered less 'political' if those fighting seem less concerned with control of government or the achievement of statehood.

The third dimension of the current Western intellectual scaffolding investigated was that of conceptions of power. Conceptions of power too were found to be compromised and altered in the transition from modernity to postmodernity: new mechanisms of power operate in a globalised world, and power no longer appears to be exercised in a linear fashion, whereby the agent with most power can readily impose its will on those with less. Under postmodern conditions power is not quantifiable in the same way: it cannot easily be determined who has the best capacity to exercise power. This is a lesson that the United States has bitterly learned in wars labelled 'asymmetrical' – a term that really signifies that the, in conventional understandings, 'weaker' side is more apt at 'exercising' power. Such 'exercise' of power takes place through the techniques of avoidance, slippage and elision, in Zygmunt Bauman's terms.

Finally, we may discern elements of a postmodern consciousness in the weakened sense of human and political agency held by the liberal world in the twenty-first century. Relative to the modern era, the contemporary liberal world appears to contend with a weaker sense of purpose, a post-teleological way in which to pursue liberal values. This altered conception of agency was shown to shore up a very particular image of the 'opponents' of policing wars – conceptualised as having little political identity or political will of their own, but instead seen to be possible to influence and persuade to accept the universalising aspirations of 'post-political' liberalism – or to be condemned as beyond the realm of politics through their 'unreasoned' or 'immoral' behaviour.

The purpose of this study has been to uncover the intellectual scaffolding, the social imaginaries and models 'by which a society interprets itself' and which sustain the contemporary liberal discourse on war.[5] In the effort to thickly describe the metaphorical imagination and narrative of war as policing, tensions in the way that 'people imagine their social existence' (in Charles Taylor's words) were uncovered in each and every one of the dimensions examined. There is, by contrast, no ambition to depict a discernible 'whole' or unity to the contemporary Western intellectual scaffolding. Instead the contradictions and tensions here described also constitute a fundamental part of what it means to live in globalised times. For Stephen Toulmin, seeking a complex whole is essential to uncovering 'cosmopolis', the relationship between 'cosmos', the order of nature, and 'polis', the order of society.[6]

The relationship between what nature 'intended' and what human beings create through will has always exercised the human imagination, Toulmin tells us. In the transition from the pre-modern to the modern period, a crisis of cosmopolis was experienced, and Europe lost 'all social, political and spiritual cohesion'.[7] Whether this is the case also today, on the brink between modernity and postmodernity, and if so in what way, is too big a question to be resolved in this book. There are, however, indications of crisis that we can clearly observe from the tensions in some of the categories we rely on to make sense of the world (time, space, power and agency). Zygmunt Bauman claims that under postmodern conditions there is an absolute absence of a 'politics of global order':

> No comparable vision has emerged so far in our times, when the modern version of ancien regime (the planet sliced into sovereign nation-states with no universal law binding them all) is falling apart. There is no 'politics of global order' in sight, boasting a vision wider than that of an average police precinct (the sole vision being the one of rounding up, incarcerating and otherwise disempowering such agents whose way of exploiting the licence made possible by the frontierland condition has been declared illegitimate).[8]

Contrary to Bauman's assertion, the liberal imagination, as we have seen, still clings to such assumptions. The view that there is, in fact, a liberal international order is a crucial component of the metaphorical understanding of war as policing. Yet if the correct conclusions have been drawn here, the view presented supports Bauman in claiming that there are fundamental tensions between the cherished view of 'international order' and the social imaginaries of our times. In other words, the policing metaphor no longer quite sustains itself. It is inherently contradictory, as we saw, for instance, in the conflicting imaginations of political space – both as supraterritorial and as tied to the modern territorial state – and these contradictions are simultaneously carried over into the understanding of war.

It is also clear from examination of four dimensions of an intellectual scaffolding or 'postmodern consciousness' – time/temporality, space/spatiality, conceptions of power and conceptions of agency – that something fundamental is changing in the current era as regards the relationship between politics, the state and the global. The relationship between the three has recurred throughout this book, not least as we have seen at various junctures how the state appears less relevant to contemporary political forces – which instead are aimed directly at the global realm. Whether we are discussing the 'policing agents' or the 'subjects' to be policed in war, this assertion holds true. It is thus clear that the relationship between politics, the state and the global is being reworked; and it is currently in a state of flux. There are, as we have seen, many indications that the state is no longer the only site of politics, nor that political action always aspires to the state, or political struggles to statehood. While I make no attempt at resolving the questions of what constitutes a *political* actor on the global scene, this book indicates some of the directions one might pursue in asking such questions. Is this then perhaps the real significance of the policing metaphor? Bauman has referred to the 'post-Panoptical era' as the era auguring '*the end of mutual engagement*: between the supervisors and the supervised, capital and labour, leaders and their followers, armies at war'.[9] So too, it seems, has the era of the metaphorical understanding of war as policing inaugurated an estrangement between opponents in war. There are fundamental differences between the US-led forces and their opponents in Iraq and Afghanistan as regards what these wars are about – and this in turn seems to be leading each side to conceive of the other as 'incomprehensible'.

Stephen Toulmin argued in *Return to Reason* (2003) that concerns about 'uncertainty, disagreement, and respect for the variety of reasonable opinions' had resurfaced.[10] The understanding of war as a tool that can effectively be used in the creation of order is a remnant of modern instrumental rationality, and it is only with hesitancy that we see decision-makers accepting the damage done to modern faith and certainty. Contrary to the modern period, which idolised stability, current belief systems idolise flexibility.[11] Profound hesitancy over what this should mean in social and political terms explains much of the tension inherent in the policing metaphor itself and in the wider discourse on war.

## Concluding thoughts

The policing logic described in this book ultimately concerns the logic of a war without antagonism. Visions of the 'post-ideological', the 'post-political' or the 'post-adversarial' have migrated from the realm of the domestic to the realm of the international and global, where 'liberal internationalism' has acquired such supremacy that the usurpation of its discriminating concept of war in international institutions is taken for granted. In its most recent reincarnation as 'counterinsurgency', where the pretence to fostering 'good govern-ance' and 'legitimacy' is constituted as central, the discourse of war as *persuasion* seems to have reached its apotheosis. The moralisation of politics described by Chantal Mouffe has featured prominently in debates about conflict since the end of the Cold War, and acceler-ated post-9/11. Yet, just as Mouffe contends as regards the domestic political sphere, the designation of political opposition and resistance as 'anti-political' or 'apolitical' does not make resistance disappear.[12] On the contrary, Mouffe argues that in the domestic setting this has pushed political opposition to the margins – exemplified best by the rise of the extreme right in Europe in this same time period – and relegated opposition away from the realm of agonistic, peaceful reso-lution of political conflict, to the realm of the violently antagonistic. This tendency is being mirrored on the global level, as evidenced in the lack of accepted political alternative to the dominant liberal inter-nationalist creed – even when this manifests itself in war-fighting. Instead, resistance in the policing logic becomes discredited as 'disor-derly', 'terrorist' or 'criminal'.

Conceptions of politics and of the political have been shown to be central to conceptions of war. In the attempt to explain, in the thickest sense, how it has come to be that policing logics took such hold in the two decades after the end of the Cold War, this book has turned to explorations of the key ideas that sustain political imagination. Drawing on themes familiar from the history of social and political thought, I have invoked the notions of time, space, power and agency. Reading the temporality and spatiality of politics and war, along with underpinning imaginations of power and agency, has shown just how widely and deeply the discourse of non-adversarial politics spread in the past two decades. Ultimately, this has come to construe 'war' as something akin to a policing enterprise: a form of 'consensual war', wherein no 'real' political opposition is acknowledged. The refusal to admit political opposition is integral to the liberal policing logic – and integral to what sustains the imagination of an unproblematic com-bining of war-fighting with the establishment of 'good governance', 'trust', 'legitimacy' and so on. Yet, at the same time, the absorption of the notion of post-adversarial politics into the conception of war has also enabled that other side of counterinsurgency: the shadow war of targeted killings carried out in secret Special Forces' operations and through the use of robotic technologies. The dramatic increase in shadow practices, combined with a perceptible lessening of interest in the costly large-scale military–civilian–humanitarian engagement that has been the story of the interventions in Iraq and Afghanistan, indicates that the policing wars described in this book are beginning to take on new forms. To properly investigate future modes and rationalisations of war, it will be equally important to investigate the social imaginaries that sustain them.

# Notes

## Introduction

1. J. Crabtree (17 Dec. 2008) 'Public intellectual of the year: David Petreaus', *Prospect Magazine*; J. Crabtree (17 Jan. 2009) 'An intellectual surge', *Prospect Magazine.*
2. L. Khalili (2010) 'The new (and old) classics of counterinsurgency', *Middle East Report*, p. 2.
3. A. Gat (2006) *War in Human Civilization* (Oxford: Oxford University Press), preface, p. xi.
4. Of the 183,000 troops in Iraq in 2005, the United States contributed 160,000. The highest number reached by the United Kingdom in Iraq was 10,000, in 2004. Stockholm International Peace Research Institute (SIPRI), Multilateral Peace Operations Database, available at URL <http://www.sipri.org/databases/pko>. International Security Assistance Force, British Army Website, URL <http://www.army.mod.uk/operations-deployments/22812.aspx>.
5. DAC (1997) *DAC Guidelines on Conflict, Peace and Development Co-operation* (Paris: Development Asssistance Committee (DAC), Organisation for Economic Co-operation and Development (OECD)); J. Solana (2003) *A Secure Europe in a Better World: European Security Strategy* (Paris: European Union Institute for Security Studies); DFID (2005) *Fighting Poverty to Build a Safer World: A Strategy for Security and* Development (London: DFID); United States Department of the Army Headquarters (December 2006) Counterinsurgency Field Manual FM 3-24. House of Commons Defence Committee, The Comprehensive Approach: the point of war is not just to win but to make better peace, 18 Mar. 2010, available at URL <http://www.publications.parliament.uk/pa/cm200910/cmselect/cmdfence/224/224.pdf>.
6. R. Stewart (9 July 2009) 'The irresistible illusion', *London Review of Books*, vol. 31, no. 3.
7. For influential accounts, see M. Duffield (2007) *Development, Security and Unending War* (Cambridge: Polity); M. Shaw (2005) *The New Western Way of War* (Cambridge: Polity); M. Dillon and J. Reid (2009) *The Liberal Way of War: Killing to Make Life Live* (Abingdon, Oxon.: Routledge).
8. T. Blair, Speech to the Labour Party Conference, Blackpool, UK, 1 October 2002, available at URL <http://www.theguardian.com/politics/2002/oct/01/labourconference.labour14>; G. W. Bush, Speech on US strategy in Iraq, delivered at the U.S. Army War College, Carlisle, Pa., 24 March 2004, available at URL <http://www.nytimes.com/2004/05/24/politics/25PTEX-FULL.html>; B. Obama, Speech on US strategy for Afghanistan and Pakistan, 27 March 2009, available at URL <http://www.cfr.org/pakistan/obamas-strategy-afghanistan-pakistan-march-2009/p18952>.

9. M. Howard (2008) 'Are we at war?', *Survival*, vol. 59, no. 4, p. 254.
10. J. Mueller (2004) *The Remnants of War* (Ithaca, NY: Cornell University Press), pp. 116, 84. See also C.S. Gray (2004) *The Sheriff: America's Defence of the New World Order* (Lexington: University Press of Kentucky).
11. Definitions used by the Uppsala Conflict Data Programme can be found at URL <http://www.pcr.uu.se/research/UCDP/data_and_publications/definitions_all.htm>.
12. M. Kaldor (1999) *New and Old Wars: Organized Violence in a Global Era* (Oxford: Polity Press); T.X. Hammes (2004) *The Sling and the Stone: On War in the 21st Century* (St Paul, MN: Zenith); F.G. Hoffman (2009) 'Hybrid warfare and challenges', *Joint Forces Quarterly*, no. 52.
13. M. Weber (1964) *The Theory of Economic and Social Organization*, trans. A.M. Henderson and Talcott Parsons (London: Collier-Macmillan).
14. A. Giddens (1985) *The Nation-State and Violence* (Los Angeles: University of California Press), p. 192.
15. For the classic discussion of a 'system' versus a 'society' of states, see H. Bull ([1977] 2002) *The Anarchical Society: A Study of Order in World Politics* (Basingstoke: Palgrave Macmillan).
16. H. Morgenthau (1973) *Politics Among Nations: The Struggle for Power and Peace* (5th edition) (New York: Alfred A. Knopf), pp. 126–30.
17. B. Greener-Barcham (2010) *The New International Policing* (Cambridge: Cambridge University Press). See also R. Dwan (ed.) (2002), *Executive Policing* (Oxford: Oxford University Press, for SIPRI) and B. Greener-Barcham (2007) 'Crossing the green or blue line? Exploring the military–police divide', *Small Wars and Insurgencies* 18, no. 1.
18. For an excellent overview of the Latin American context, see K. Koonings and D. Kruijt (eds) (2004), *Armed Actors: Organized Violence and State Failure in Latin America* (London and New York: Zed Books).
19. P. Andreas and E. Nadelmann (2006) *Policing the Globe: Criminalization and Crime Control in International Relations* (Oxford: Oxford University Press).
20. M. Hardt and A. Negri (2000) *Empire* (Cambridge, MA: Harvard University Press). The relationship between war and policing has also been addressed in M. Dean (2009) *Governmentality: Power and Rule in Modern Society* (Thousand Oaks, CA.: Sage); M. Dubber and M. Valverde (eds) (2007) *The New Police Science: The Police Power in Domestic and International Governance* (Stanford, CA.: Stanford University Press); D. Bigo (2005) *Policing Insecurity Today* (New York, NY.: Palgrave Macmillan). See also J. Bachmann, C. Bell and C. Holmqvist (eds) (forthcoming 2014) *WAR:POLICE: Assemblages of Intervention* (London: Routledge).
21. C. von Clausewitz (2008) *On War*, edited and abridged by B. Heuser (London: Penguin), p. 1.
22. T. Barkawi and S. Brighton (2011) 'Powers of war: fighting, knowledge, and critique', *International Political Sociology*, vol. 5, p. 136.
23. Quoted in R. Stewart (2009) 'The irresistible illusion', *London Review of Books*.
24. Bertrand Russell, quoted in M. Black (1962) *Models and Metaphors: Studies in Language and Philosophy* (Ithaca, NY: Cornell University Press), p. 1.

25. A. Williams (2003), 'Introduction' in P. Mandaville and A. Williams (eds), *Meaning and International Relations* (London: Routledge), p. 3. See also P.L. Berger and T. Luckmann (1967) *The Social Construction of Reality* (London: Allen Lane) and J. R. Searle (1995) *The Social Construction of Reality* (New York: Free Press).
26. A. Blok (2000), 'The enigma of senseless violence', in G. Aijmer and J. Abbink (eds) *Meanings of Violence: A Cross-Cultural Perspective* (Oxford and New York: Berg), pp. 23–4.
27. Ibid., p. 24.
28. Aijmer and Abbink, *Meanings of Violence*, p. xiii.
29. Online etymology dictionary URL <http://www.etymonline.com/index. php>.
30. G. Lakoff and M. Johnson (2003) *Metaphors We Live By*, Revised ed. (Chicago: Chicago University Press). See also G. Lakoff and M. Johnson (1999) *Philosophy in the Flesh: The Embodied Mind and its Challenge to Western Thought* (New York: Basic Books).
31. Lakoff and Johnson, *Metaphors We Live By*, pp. 3–5. See also Black, *Models and Metaphors*; B. Diemert (2005) 'Uncontainable metaphor: George F. Kennan's "X" article and Cold War discourse', *Canadian Review of American Studies* 35, no. 1, p. 24.
32. Lakoff and Johnson, *Metaphors We Live By*, p. 4.
33. Black, Models and Metaphors, pp. 39–40.
34. F.A. Beer and C. de Landtsheer (eds) (2004) *Metaphorical World Politics* (East Lansing, MI: Michigan State University Press), p. 24.
35. Vico quoted in Paul Chilton (1996) *Security Metaphors: Cold War Discourse from Containment to Common House* (New York: Lang. cop.) p. 39. See also Beer and Landtsheer, *Metaphorical World Politics*, pp. 24–5.
36. S. Toulmin (1992) *Cosmopolis: The Hidden Agenda of Modernity* (Chicago: University of Chicago Press), p. 22.
37. Beer and Landtsheer, *Metaphorical World Politics*, pp. 24–5.
38. Geertz quoted in Beer and Landtsheer, *Metaphorical World Politics*, p. 14; Chilton *Security Metaphors: Cold War Discourse from Containment to Common House*, p. 26.
39. R. Paris (2002) 'Kosovo and the metaphor war', *Political Science Quarterly*, vol. 117, no. 3 pp. 425–6.
40. D. Armstrong and T. Farrell (2005) 'Force and legitimacy in world politics', *Review of International Studies* 31, pp. 10–12.
41. J.A. Lynn (2003) *Battle: A History of Combat and Culture* (Boulder, CO: Westview Press).
42. T. Farrell (2005) *The Norms of War: Cultural Beliefs and Modern Conflict* (Boulder, CO: Lynne Rienner), pp. 1, 178. See also M. Finnemore (2003) *The Purpose of Intervention: Changing Beliefs About the Use of Force* (Ithaca, NY: Cornell University Press).
43. Shaw (2005) *The New Western Way of War*, p. 1.
44. International Human Rights and Conflict Resolution Clinic, Stanford Law School & Global Justice Clinic NYU School of Law (2012) *Living Under Drones*.

45. N. Rengger (2005) 'The judgement of war: on the idea of legitimate force in world politics', *Review of International Studies* vol. 31, S.1, p. 146.
46. Especially C. Schmitt (2011) *Writings on War*, Edited and translated by T. Nunan (Cambridge: Polity)
47. Toulmin, *Cosmopolis*, p. 116.
48. Ibid., 116.
49. Ibid., pp. 108, 109–16.
50. Ibid., 116.
51. Ibid., p. 117–123.
52. C. Taylor (2004) *Modern Social Imaginaries* (Durham, NC and London: Duke University Press), p. 23.
53. Ibid., p. 25.
54. G. Delanty (2000) Modernity and Postmodernity: Knowledge, Power and the Self (London: Sage Publications), p. xi.
55. Heraclitus, ca. 540–475 BC.

# 1 Narratives of Disorder

1. United Nations (1992) 'An agenda for peace: preventive diplomacy, peacemaking and peace-keeping', Report of the Secretary-General pursuant to the statement adopted by the Summit Meeting of the Security Council on 31 Jan. 1992.
2. Speech by President William J. Clinton, 'Speech by the President at the Bosnia–Croat Peace Agreement Signing', 18 Mar. 1994, URL: <http://www.clintonfoundation.org/legacy/031894-speech-by-president-at-bosnia-croat-peace-agreement-signing.htm>.
3. Speech by Prime Minister Tony Blair, 'Doctrine of the International Community', at the Economic Club, Chicago, 24 Apr. 1999, URL: <http://www.number10.gov.uk/output/Page1297.asp>.
4. According to data presented by the Uppsala Conflict Data Programme, only four of the 57 conflicts between 1990 and 2005 were inter-state conflicts. Lotta Harbom and Peter Wallensteen, 'Appendix 2A: Patterns of major armed conflicts, 1990–2005' in Stockholm International Peace Research Institute (SIPRI), ed., *SIPRI Yearbook 2006: Armaments, disarmament and international security* (Oxford: Oxford University Press, 2006).
5. M. Kaldor (1999) *New and Old Wars: Organized Violence in a Global Era* (Cambridge: Polity Press). See also H. Münkler (2005) *The New Wars*, trans. Patrick Camiller (Cambridge: Polity Press).
6. For critiques of Kaldor, see M. Berdal (2003) 'How "new" are "new wars"? Global economic change and the study of civil war', *Global Governance 9*, no. 4; S.N. Kalyvas (2001) '"New" and "old" civil wars – a valid distinction?" *World Politics* 54, no. 1; E. Newman (2004) 'The "new wars" debate: a historical perspective is needed', *Security Dialogue* 35, no. 2.
7. E. Luttwak (1999) 'Give war a chance', *Foreign Affairs* 78, no. 4.
8. British troops sent to Sierra Leone in 2000 were an exception to this general trend. Details of individual troop contributions by country can be

found in the 'peace operations' database of the Stockholm International Peace Research Institute, publicly available at URL <http://www.sipri.org/databases/pko>.

9.  G.B. Helman and S.R. Ratner (1992) 'Saving failed states', *Foreign Policy* 89, Winter, p. 3.

10.  I.W. Zartman (ed.) (1995) *Collapsed States: The Disintegration and Restoration of Legitimate Authority* (Boulder, CO: Lynne Rienner), p. 1. See also J. Herbst (1997) 'Responding to state failure in Africa', *International Security* 21, pp. 120–44.

11.  Helman and Ratner, 'Saving failed states', p. 3.

12.  Ibid.

13.  For an example of the former view, see K. Menkhaus (2004) *Somalia: State Collapse and the Threat of Terrorism*, Adelphi Papers (London: Routledge, for IISS); and for an example of the latter, see W. Reno (1998) *Warlord Politics and African States* (Boulder, CO: Lynne Rienner).

14.  R. Marchal (2007) 'Warlordism and terrorism: how to obscure an already confusing crisis? The case of Somalia', *International Affairs* 83, no. 6, p. 1094.

15.  Menkhaus, *Somalia*, pp. 32–3.

16.  T. Lyons and A.I. Samatar (1995) *Somalia: State Collapse, Multilateral Intervention, and Strategies for Political Reconstruction* (Washington, DC: Brookings Institution), quoted in T. Langford (1999) 'Things fall apart: state failure and the politics of intervention', *International Studies Review* 1, no. 1, p. 61.

17.  C. Hughes and V. Pupavac (2005) 'Framing post-conflict societies: international pathologisation of Cambodia and the post-Yugoslav states', *Third World Quarterly* 26, no. 6.

18.  C. Hedges (2002) *War Is a Force that Gives Us Meaning* (Oxford: Public Affairs Ltd).

19.  Helman and Ratner, 'Saving failed states'. See also A. Mazrui (1994) 'Decaying parts of Africa need benign colonization', *International Herald Tribune*, 4 Aug.

20.  Helman and Ratner, 'Saving failed states'.

21.  For an account of how the concept has evolved, see R.H. Dorff (2005) 'Failed states after 9/11: what did we know and what have we learned?' *International Studies Perspective* vol. 6. 'State fragility' has been used to denote a combination of a lack of capacity and a lack of resilience on the part of states. R. Picciotto, F. Olonisakin and M. Clarke (2007) *Global Development and Human Security* (New Brunswick, NJ: Transaction Publishers).

22.  R.D. Kaplan (1994) 'The coming anarchy: how scarcity, crime, overpopulation, tribalism, and disease are rapidly destroying the social fabric of our planet', *Atlantic Monthly*, Feb. See also R.D. Kaplan (1993) *Balkan Ghosts: A Journey Through History* (New York: St Martin's Press); R.D. Kaplan (1996) *The Ends of the Earth: From Togo to Turkmenistan, From Iran to Cambodia – A Journey to the Frontiers of Anarchy* (New York: Vintage Press).

23.  Kaplan, 'The coming anarchy', p. 3.

24. Emphasis added. Kaplan, 'The coming anarchy'.

25. 'Neo-medievalism was another in vogue term at the time, see e.g. C. Berzins and P. Cullen (2003) 'Terrorism and neo-medievalism', *Civil Wars* 6, no. 2.

26. M. Duffield (2001) *Global Governance and the New Wars: The Merging of Security and Development* (London: Zed Books), pp. 109–13. T. Homer-Dixon, J. Boutwell and G. Rathjens (1993) 'Environmental scarcity and violent conflict', *Scientific American*, Feb., pp. 38–45.

27. M. Ignatieff (1998) *The Warrior's Honour: Ethnic War and the Modern Conscience* (New York: Metropolitan Books). For further critique of the concept of ethnic conflict, see D. Campbell (1998) *National Deconstruction: Violence, Identity and Justice in Bosnia* (Minneapolis, MN: University of Minneapolis Press).

28. A. Lieven (1998) *Chechnya: Tombstone of Russian Power* (New Haven and London: Yale University Press), p. 110.

29. For illuminating discussions, see Ignatieff, *The Warrior's Honour*; S. Woodward (1995) *Balkan Tragedy: Chaos and Dissolution After the Cold War* (Washington. DC: Brookings Institution).

30. S.P. Huntington (1996) *The Clash of Civilizations and the Remaking of World Order* (London: The Free Press, Simon and Schuster UK Ltd), Preface.

31. Huntington, *Clash of Civilizations*, p. 47. S.P. Huntington (1993) 'The clash of civilizations?' *Foreign Affairs* 72, no. 3, p. 27.

32. Huntington, *Clash of Civilizations*, pp. 40–8, Huntington, 'The clash of civilizations?', p. 25.

33. Emphasis in original. Huntington, 'The clash of civilizations?', p. 29.

34. Ibid., p. 27.

35. For Sen it is the *illusion* of identity rather than identity per se that is the operating factor. Amartya Sen, *Identity and Violence: The Illusion of Destiny* (London: Allen Lane, 2006).

36. P. Collier and A. Hoeffler (2000) *Greed and grievance in civil wars*, Policy Research Working Paper 2355 (The World Bank Development Research Group). See also P. Collier (2000) 'Doing well out of war', in M. Berdal and D. Malone (eds) *Greed and Grievance: Economic Agendas in Civil Wars* (Boulder, CO: Lynne Rienner).

37. Collier, 'Doing well out of war', pp. 94–6.

38. Ibid., pp. 97–9.

39. C. Cramer (2002) '*Homo economicus* goes to war: methodological individualism, rational choice and the political economy of conflict', *World Development* 30, no. 11.

40. Collier, 'Doing well out of war', in Berdal and Malone (eds) *Greed and Grievance*, p. 92.

41. Cramer, '*Homo economicus* goes to war', p. 1857.

42. D. Keen (2000) 'Incentives and disincentives for violence', in Berdal and Malone (eds) *Greed and Grievance*. See also Cramer, '*Homo economicus* goes to war';, D. Keen (1998) *The Economic Functions of Violence in Civil Wars*, Adelphi Papers (Oxford: Oxford University Press on behalf of the IISS).

43. D. Keen and M. Berdal (1997) 'Violence and economic agendas in civil wars: some policy implications', *Millennium* 26, no. 3, pp. 798–9.

44. Ibid., p. 799.

45. Ibid., pp. 797, 800.

46. K. Ballentine and J. Sherman (eds) (2003) *The Political Economy of Armed Conflict: Beyond Greed and Grievance* (Boulder, CO: Lynne Rienner). See also M. Berdal (2005) 'Beyond greed and grievance – and not too soon …A review essay', *Review of International Studies* 31.

47. Compare also Keen, *The Economic Functions of Violence in Civil Wars*, and D. Keen (2005) *Conflict and Collusion in Sierra Leone* (Oxford: James Curry). In the latter, Keen places more emphasis than previously on the role played by 'psychological functions', especially the role of emotions such as shame and humiliation (both on the part of rebels and government forces) in producing and sustaining violence. See esp. pp. 48–55 and pp. 56–81.

48. For a discussion of Philip Windsor's critique of positivist thought, see M. Berdal (2002) '"A cross-roads rather than an academic discipline" – Philip Windsor and the study of International Relations', in P. Windsor and M. Berdal (eds) *Studies in International Relations: Essays by Philip Windsor* (Brighton: Sussex Academic Press), pp. 3–6.

49. Blok, 'The enigma of senseless violence'.

50. J. Mueller (2004) *The Remnants of War* (Ithaca, NY: Cornell University Press).

51. Ibid.

52. Ibid., p. 92.

53. Ibid., p. 99. See also P. Gourevitch (1998) *We Wish to Inform You that Tomorrow We Will Be Killed with Our Families: Stories from Rwanda* (New York: Farrar, Straus and Giroux). Chris Hedges struck a similar note when he wrote that the warlords in the former republic of Yugoslavia were 'made up of the dregs of Yugoslav society … thieves, embezzlers, petty thugs'. C. Hedges (2002) *War Is a Force that Gives Us Meaning* (New York: Perseus Books), p. 27.

54. Mueller, *The Remnants of War*, pp. 100–7.

55. Ibid., pp. 83–4. Mueller does admit that some contemporary civil wars may be seen as 'disciplined' (interestingly, he cites Afghanistan, the first Chechen war, Lebanese civil war and Sri Lanka, though it is not clear how this fits together with his general thesis). See also Mueller, *The Remnants of War*, pp. 107–9.

56. Ibid., p. 116.

57. Ibid., p. 140.

58. Ibid., p. 84.

59. Ibid., p. 149.

60. Alex Schmid's (1988) study comparing a vast number of academic definitions of terrorism finds that the second most common feature (in 65 percent) of terrorism cited was that the violence was 'political'. See A.P. Schmid, A.J. Jongman et al. (1988) *Political Terrorism: A New*

*Guide to Actors, Authors, Concepts, Databases, Theories and Literature* (New Brunswick, NJ: Transaction), pp. 5–6.

61. See, for example, R. Shultz and A. Dew (2006) *Insurgents, Terrorists and Militias: The Warriors of Contemporary Combat* (New York: Columbia University Press).

62. For an example of this view, see A.K. Cronin (2006) 'How al-Qaeda ends: the decline and demise of terrorist groups', *International Security* 31, no. 1.

63. I. Duyvesteyn (2004) 'How new is the new terrorism?', *Studies in Conflict and Terrorism* 27, p. 443. See also W. Laqueur (2004) *No End to War* (New York: Continuum).

64. M.B. Salter (2002) *Barbarians and Civilisation in International Relations* (London: Pluto Press), esp. pp. 128–56.

65. C.R. Browning (1998) *Ordinary Men: Reserve Police Battalion 101 and the Final Solution in Poland* (New York: HarperCollins).

66. J. Wilhelmsen (2005) 'Between a rock and a hard place: the islamisation of the Chechen separatist movement', *Europe-Asia Studies* 57, no. 1.

67. US Department of State official website, 'Foreign Terrorist Organizations', Office of the Co-ordinator for Counter-Terrorism, 19 Jan. 2010, URL <http://www.state.gov/s/ct/rls/other/des/123085.htm>, accessed 30 Apr. 2010; UK Home Office official website, 'Proscribed terrorist organisations', Office for Security and Counter Terrorism, URL <http://security.homeoffice.gov.uk/terrorist-threat/proscribed-terrorist-orgs/>, accessed 20 Apr. 2010; and Official Journal of the European Union, Council Common Position 2009/67/CFSP, 26 Jan. 2009, URL <http://eur-lex.europa.eu/LexUriServ/LexUriServ.do?uri=OJ:L:2009:023:0037:0042:EN:PDF>, accessed 30 Apr. 2010.

68. The list was established under UN Security Council Resolution 1373 (2001), which also envisages a Counter Terrorism Committee (CTC) to oversee its implementation. Available at URL <http://www.un.org/News/Press/docs/2001/sc7158.doc.htm>, accessed 28 Apr. 2010.

69. Kaldor, *New and Old Wars*, p. 5.

70. M.V. Rasmussen (2006) *The Risk Society at War: Terror, Technology and Strategy in the Twenty-First Century* (Cambridge: Cambridge University Press), p. 10.

71. R. Cooper (2000) *The Post-modern State and the World Order* (London: Demos, 2000).

72. The literature on state-building is vast. For two influential works on the topic, see S. Chesterman (2004) *You, the People: The United Nations, Transitional Administration and State-Building* (Oxford: Oxford University Press); and R.I. Rotberg (ed.) (2004) *When States Fail: Causes and Consequences* (Princeton: Princeton University Press), pp. 151–302.

73. OECD Development Assistance Committee (DAC) (2004) 'Security Sector Reform and Governance: Policy and Good Practice' (OECD: Paris), pp. 16–18.

74. 'An agenda for peace: preventive diplomacy, peacemaking and peacekeeping (Report of the Secretary-General pursuant to the statement adopted by the Summit Meeting of the Security Council on 31 Jan. 1992)'.

75. Campbell,, *National Deconstruction.*
76. D. Campbell (1992) 'Apartheid cartography: the political anthropology and spatial effects of international diplomacy in Bosnia', *Political Geography* 18, p. 402.
77. W. Posch (2005) 'A majority ignored: the Arabs in Iraq', in W. Posch (ed.) *Looking Into Iraq*, Chaillot Paper (Paris: ISS), p. 26. See also T. Dodge (2005) *Iraq's Future: The Aftermath of Regime Change* (London: Routledge, for IISS).
78. For an overview of some of the most important initiatives in this regard, see M. Taylor and A. Huser (2003) *Security, Development and Economies of Conflict: Problems and Responses*, Fafo AIS Policy Brief (Oslo: Fafo); N. Tschirgi (2003) *Peacebuilding as the Link between Security and Development: Is the Window of Opportunity Closing?*, IPA Studies in Security and Development (New York: International Peace Academy).
79. Berdal, 'Beyond greed and grievance', p. 689.
80. The Kimberley Process designed to combat trade in 'conflict diamonds' is one example of this type of policy. See URL <http://www.kimberleyprocess. com/>, accessed 28 Apr. 2010.
81. To name but a few: Challenges and Change High-level Panel on Threats, 'A more secure world: our shared responsibility', Report of the High-level Panel on Threats, Challenges and Change, UN documents, A/59/565, 4 Dec. 2004 (United Nations, 2004); *A Secure Europe in a Better World: European Security Strategy* (Paris: European Union Institute for Security Studies (EUISS), 2003); *Quadrennial Defense Review 2006* (Washington, DC: US Department of Defense, 2006).
82. For a pro-integration view of counter-terrorism and development, see K. von Hippel (2006) *Counter-radicalization Development Assistance*, Danish Institute for International Studies (DIIS) Working Paper (Copenhagen: DIIS). For a critical view, see J. Beall, T. Goodfellow and J. Putzel (2006) 'Introductory article: on the discourse of terrorism, security and development', *Journal of International Development* 18.
83. R. Paris (2002) 'International peacebuilding and the "mission civilisatrice"', *Review of International Studies* 28, no. 4; and R. Paris (2003) 'Peacekeeping and the constraints of global culture', *European Journal of International Relations* 9, no. 3.
84. Duffield, *Development, Security and Unending War.*
85. J. Mayall (2007) 'The new interventionism', in M. Berdal and S. Economides (eds) *United Nations Interventionism, 1991–2004* (Cambridge: Cambridge University Press).

# 2   Perpetual Policing Wars

1. M. Van Creveld (2006) *The Changing Face of War: Lessons of Combat, from the Marne to Iraq* (New York: Ballantine Books), Introduction, p. ix.
2. Ibid., Introduction, p. x.

3. J. Mueller (2004) *The Remnants of War* (Ithaca, NY: Cornell University Press), p. 22.
4. Ibid., p. 119.
5. Ibid., pp. 119, 22.
6. D. Keen (2007) *Endless War? Hidden Functions of the 'War on Terror'* (London: Pluto Press), p. 3.
7. Ibid.
8. Ibid.
9. *Quadrennial Defense Review 2006.* President Barack Obama has since attempted to change the language of the 'war on terror', referring instead to 'overseas contingency operations'. S. Wilson and Al Kamen (2009), '"Global war on terror" is given new name', *Washington Post* (25 Mar.).
10. Bauman considers five of 'zombie categories' in his *Liquid Modernity* (emancipation, individuality, time/space, work and community), out of which the relationship between time and space is held to be most important. Z. Bauman (2000) *Liquid Modernity* (Cambridge: Polity Press), p. 8.
11. M. Castells (1996), *The Rise of the Network Society (The Information Age: Economy, Society and Culture. Vol. 1)* (Oxford: Blackwell Publishers), p. 407.
12. K. Hutchings (2008) *Time and World Politics: Thinking the Present* (Manchester: Manchester University Press).
13. A. Heller (1999) *A Theory of Modernity* (Oxford: Blackwell Publishers), p. 11.
14. P. Hassner (1987) 'Immanuel Kant 1724–1804', in L. Strauss and J. Cropsey (eds) *History of Political Philosophy* (Chicago: Chicago University Press, 3rd edn), p. 592.
15. Ibid.
16. I. Kant (1784) 'What is enlightenment?', Köningsberg.
17. Ibid., pp. 595–6.
18. J. Gray (2003) *Al Qaeda and What It Means to Be Modern* (London: Faber and Faber), pp. 101–2.
19. Ibid., p. 101.
20. Ibid., p. 102.
21. Berlin, quoted in Z. Laïdi (1998) *A World Without Meaning: The Crisis of Meaning in International Politics* (London: Routledge), p. 12.
22. Ibid., p. 1.
23. Ibid.
24. Heller, *A Theory of Modernity*, p. 7.
25. Ibid.
26. Bauman, *Liquid Modernity*, p. 29.
27. Heller, *A Theory of Modernity*, p. 7.
28. C. Coker (1998) *War and the Illiberal Conscience* (Oxford: Westview).
29. Ibid., p. 39.
30. Ibid.
31. Ibid.
32. Bauman, *Liquid Modernity*, pp. 15, 118.
33. (My emphasis.) Heller, *A Theory of Modernity*, p. 183.

34. Castells, *The Rise of the Network Society*, p. 407.
35. Castells, 'Materials for an exploratory theory of the network society', ibid., p. 13.
36. Laïdi, *A World Without Meaning*, pp. 11–14.
37. Bauman, *Liquid Modernity*, pp. 1–15.
38. Ibid., p. 6.
39. M. Foucault ([1977] 1991) *Discipline and Punish: The Birth of the Prison* (London: Penguin). The topic of power is treated in Chapter 4.
40. Bauman, *Liquid Modernity*, pp. 11–13.
41. Ibid., p. 2.
42. Castells, *The Rise of the Network Society*, p. 406.
43. Perhaps the best overview of the intermingling of military and police practices is found in B.K. Greener (2009) *The New International Policing* (Basingstoke: Palgrave Macmillan).
44. See, for example, J. Lynn (2003) *Battle: A History of Combat and Culture* (New York: Westview), pp. 111–44.
45. R. Smith (2005) *The Utility of Force: The Art of War in the Modern World* (London: Allen Lane), p. 1.
46. For the full text of Bush's 'end of major combat operations' speech delivered on 2 May 2003 on board the USS *Abraham Lincoln* off the coast of California, see URL <http://news.bbc.co.uk/1/hi/world/americas/2994345.stm>. See also G. Rachman (2008) 'Too soon to give up in Afghanistan', *Financial Times*, 12 Feb.
47. See, for example, H. Kissinger (2005) 'Lessons for an exit strategy', *Washington Post* 12 Aug.; B. Posen (2006) 'Exit strategy: how to disengage from Iraq in 18 months', *Boston Review*, Jan./Feb.
48. C. von Clausewitz (1976) *On War*, ed. and trans. M. Howard and P. Paret, abridged by Beatrice Heuser (Oxford: Oxford University Press [Princeton University Press 1976], abridged version 2007), p. 28.
49. Ibid., p. 29.
50. von Clausewitz, *On War*, especially Book One and Book Eight.
51. P. Windsor (2002) *Strategic Thinking: An Introduction and Farewell* (Boulder, CO: Lynne Rienner Publishers), p. 29.
52. The purpose here is not to assess the legitimacy or otherwise of any of these reasons, merely to point to that fact that there was little certainty over what exactly the purpose of the war was. This of course made any discussion of whether the war was legitimate or not hopelessly subjective. For detail on the Blair government's focus on *how* the invasion of Iraq should be conducted (persuading the US to take the UN route) rather than *why*, see A. Seldon, P. Snowdon and D. Collings (2007) *Blair Unbound* (London: Simon & Schuster Ltd), pp. 80–170.
53. *Quadrennial Defense Review 2006*.
54. Quoted in Bauman, *Liquid Modernity*, p. 102.
55. Quoted in Laïdi, *A World Without Meaning*, p. 79.
56. See, for example, C. Coker (2001) *Humane Warfare* (London: Routledge) and T. Farrell (2005) *The Norms of War: Cultural Beliefs and Modern Conflict* Boulder, CO: Lynne Rienner Publishers).

57. For a wider discussion, see T. Edmunds (2006) 'What *are* the armed forces for? The changing nature of militaries in Europe', *International Affairs* 82, no. 6; C. Brown (2006) 'Conceptions of a rule-governed international order: Europe vs. America?' *International Relations* 20, no. 3; and M. Duffield (2007) *Development, Security and Unending War: Governing the World of Peoples* (London: Polity Press).

58. Smith, *The Utility of Force*, p. 16.

59. P. Cornish (2009) 'The United States and counterinsurgency: "political first, political last, political always"', *International Affairs* 85, no. 1, p. 74.

60. A point made by M. Dillon and J. Read (2009) *The Liberal Way of War: Killing to Make Life Live* (Abingdon: Routledge), and Duffield, *Development, Security and Unending War*.

61. RUSI Report from Conference 'Transformation of Military Operations on the Cusps', 14–15 Mar. 2005. Available at URL <www.rusi.org/downloads/assets/Conference_Report.doc>.

62. Force protection is sufficiently paramount for Western militaries for Smith to consider it one of six key features of 'war amongst the people', what he posits as the contemporary paradigm for Western war. Smith, *The Utility of Force*, p. 17.

63. Y.-K. Heng (2006) *War as Risk Management: Strategy and Conflict in an Age of Globalised Risks*, Contemporary Security Series (Abingdon: Routledge); M. Rasmussen (2006) *The Risk Society at War: Terror, Technology and Strategy in the Twenty-First Century*. (Cambridge: Cambridge University Press). There are important critiques of these authors' use of Beck's theories of risk – see, for instance, C. Aradau and R. Van Munster (2007) 'Governing terrorism through risk: taking precautions, (un)knowing the future', *European Journal of International Relations* 13, no. 1, pp. 89–115. The discussion here however focuses on the policy-proximate interpretations of risk, which largely follow Rasmussen's.

64. Heng, *War as Risk Management*, p. 34.

65. United States Department of Defense (2001), *Quadrennial Defense Review Report*. Available at URL <http://www.defense.gov/pubs/qdr2001.pdf>.

66. For a general discussion of the essentialising powers of 'naming', see M.V. Bhatia (ed.) (2007) *Terrorism and the Politics of Naming* (New York: Routledge). This can be seen not only in Afghanistan and Iraq; see also Wilhelmsen's discussion of Chechnya in J. Wilhelmsen (2005) 'Between a rock and a hard place: the islamisation of the Chechen separatist movement', *Europe-Asia Studies* 57, no. 1.

67. 'The President's State of the Union Address', 29 Jan. 2002, The United States Capitol, Washington, DC, URL: <http://www.whitehouse.gov/news/releases/2002/01/20020129-11.html>, accessed 28 Apr. 2010.

68. C. Tilly (2004) 'Terror, terrorism, terrorists', *Sociological Theory* 22, no. 1.

69. John Reid, UK Home Secretary, Statement taken from 'Home Secretary to Ban Terror Groups', Home Office Press Release, 26 July 2006. Available at URL <http://press.homeoffice.gov.uk/press-releases/Commencement-of-New-Terrorism-Po?version=1>, accessed 28 Apr. 2010.

70. For detail on the contemporary international human right regime, see C. Brown (2002) *Sovereignty, Rights and Justice: International Political Theory Today* (Cambridge: Polity Press), esp. chapter 7. For discussion of different positions in recent debates on the relationship between liberty, security and justice, see e.g. T. Meisels (2005) 'How terrorism upsets liberty', *Political Studies* 53, no. 1.

71. BBC World News Online 'Colombian "killings" shake army', 25 Oct. 2008, URL: <http://news.bbc.co.uk/2/hi/americas/7690490.stm>, accessed 28 Apr. 2010.

72. C. Coker (1998) *War and the Illiberal Conscience* (Boulder, CO: Westview), p. xiv.

73. H. Arendt (1966) *Origins of Totalitarianism* (New York: Harcourt Brace Jovanovich).

74. J. Butler (2004) *Precarious Life: The Powers of Mourning and Life* (London: Verso), p. 8.

75. U. Eco (2007) *Turning Back the Clock*, trans. Alastair McEwen (London: Harvill Secker).

76. Ibid., p. 26.

77. Ibid.

78. D. Filkins (2009) 'Stanley McChrystal's Long War', *New York Times*, 14 Oct.

79. Rumsfeld, quoted in Bauman, *Liquid Modernity*, p. 102.

80. L. Freedman (2005) 'The age of liberal wars', *Review of International Studies* 31, p. 94.

81. Ibid., p. 98.

82. C. Coker (2008) *Ethics and War in the 21st Century*, LSE International Studies (London: Routledge).

83. United States (US) Department of the Army and Department of the Navy Headquarters, US Counterinsurgency Manual (Field Manual 3-24, Marine Corps Warfighting Publication 3-33.5), Dec. 2006, A-7; Cornish, 'The United States and counterinsurgency', p. 71.

84. Cornish, 'The United States and counterinsurgency', p. 63.

# 3  Policing the Globe

1. J. Scholte (2005) *Globalisation: a Critical Introduction*, 2nd edn (London: Palgrave Macmillan), p. 4.

2. P. Hirst (2005) *Space and Power: Politics, War and Architecture* (Cambridge: Polity Press), p. 52.

3. Scholte, *Globalisation: a Critical Introduction*, p. 60.

4. C. von Clausewitz (2007) *On War*, edited and abridged by Beatrice Heuser (Oxford: Oxford University Press).

5. S. Toulmin (1992) *Cosmopolis: The Hidden Agenda of Modernity* (Chicago: Chicago University Press), p. 96.

6. N. Brenner et al. (eds) (2003) *State/Space: A Reader* (Oxford: Blackwell Publishers), p. 2. For further discussion, see I. Loader and N. Walker (2007) *Civilizing Security* (Cambridge: Cambridge University Press).

7. Toulmin, *Cosmopolis*.
8. Ibid., p. 69.
9. Loader and Walker, *Civilizing Security*, p. 35.
10. Ibid., p. 43.
11. Q. Skinner (1989) 'The state', in T. Ball, J. Farr and R.L. Hanson (eds) *Political Innovation and Conceptual Change* (Cambridge: Cambridge University Press), p. 12.
12. M. Weber (1978) *Economy and Society: An Outline of Interpretative Sociology* (Berkeley: University of California Press), p. 56. See also G. Poggi (2006) *Weber: A Short Introduction* (Cambridge: Routledge), p. 90; and (1946) 'Politics as a vocation' in H. Gerth and C. Wright Mills (eds) *From Max Weber: Essays in Sociology* (New York: Oxford University Press).
13. Scholte (2005), p. 59; Hirst, *Space and Power*, p. 27.
14. '... the claim of the modern state to monopolize the use of force is as essential to it as its character of compulsory jurisdiction and of continuous operation'. Weber, *Economy and Society*, p. 56.
15. Brenner et al., *State/Space*, p. 2.
16. M. Mann (2003) 'The autonomous power of the state: its origins, mechanisms and results', in N. Brenner et al. (eds) *State/Space*, p. 53.
17. Ibid., p. 60. Emphasis in original.
18. '[W]hen it came to questioning the self-evidence of the new world view, or disputing its right to "go without saying", the centralized nation-states proved the least hospitable environment for such discussions.' Toulmin, *Cosmopolis*, p. 123.
19. John Agnew, quoted in Brenner et al., *State/Space*, p. 2.
20. B.S. Turner (ed.) (1990) *Theories of Modernity and Postmodernity* (London: Sage Publications), p. 4.
21. C. Tilly (1990) *Coercion, Capital and European States, A.D. 990–1990* (Cambridge, MA: Basil Blackwell); C. Tilly (1985) 'War making and state making as organized crime', in P.B. Evans, D. Rueschemeyer and T. Skocpol (eds) *Bringing the State Back In* (Cambridge: Cambridge University Press).
22. Emphasis in original. The modern state was involved in four essential activities, according to Tilly, each corresponding to a form of organisation peculiar to the modern era: in the first place, the activity of 'war-making', which in organisational terms corresponded with the formation of armies, navies and supporting services. Second, 'state-making' – coterminous with the development of instruments of surveillance and control of the population within the given geographical territory. Third, Tilly cites the activity of 'protection' (reliant on war-making and state-making but with the addition of other organisational structures in the form of courts and representative assemblies); and fourth, 'extraction' (associated with the establishment of fiscal and accounting structures). Tilly, 'War making and state making as organized crime', p. 172.
23. In this vein, of course, military sociologists over the years have continued to emphasise the significance of national conscription for war.

See C. Dandeker (1990) *Surveillance, Power and Modernity: Bureaucracy and Discipline from 1700 to the Present Day* (Cambridge: Polity Press), and various contributions in C. Moskos, J. A. Williams and D.R. Segal (eds) (2000) *The Postmodern Military: Armed Forces after the Cold War* (Oxford and New York: Oxford University Press).

24. J. Lynn (2003) *Battle: A History of Combat and Culture* (Boulder, CO: Westview Press), pp. 111–44.
25. Ibid., p. 114.
26. Ibid., p. 115.
27. For Lynn the soldier's uniform is 'a metaphor for other military aspects of the ancien régime'. Ibid., pp. 117–18.
28. Ibid., p. 119.
29. Ibid., pp. 130–1.
30. Ibid., p. 143.
31. Rupert Smith's discussion of Napoleon emphasises this same precept: decisive destruction of an opposing force. R. Smith (2005) *The Utility of Force: The Art of War in the Modern World* (London: Penguin), pp. 29–63. See also A. Gat (2001) *A History of Military Thought: From the Enlightenment to the Cold War* (Oxford: Oxford University Press).
32. This categorisation is used in the Uppsala Conflict Data Programme at Uppsala University, Sweden, a leading institution in terms of quantitative research on war. For definitions, see URL <http://www.pcr.uu.se/research/ucdp/definitions/definition_of_armed_conflict/>.
33. Z. Bauman and K. Tester (2001) *Conversations with Zygmunt Bauman* (Cambridge: Polity Press), p. 139. Also quoted in Loader and Walker, *Civilizing Security*, p. 24.
34. S. Strange (1996) *The Retreat of the State: The Diffusion of Power in the World Economy* (Cambridge: Cambridge University Press). For another early contribution to the debate, see T. Risse-Kappen (ed.) (1995) *Bringing Transnational Relations Back In: Non-State Actors, Domestic Structures and International Institutions* (Cambridge: Cambridge University Press).
35. Saskia Sassen is interested in this both/and quality, considering the way 'spatial and temporal frames ... *simultaneously* inhabit national structures and are distinct from national spatial and temporal frames as these have been historically constructed'. Emphasis in original. S. Sassen (2006) *Territory, Authority, Rights: From Medieval to Global Assemblages* (Oxford and Princeton: Princeton University Press), p. 23.
36. Ibid., p. 3. J.A. Scholte (2008) 'Defining globalization', *The World Economy* 31, pp. 1478–93.
37. Scholte, 'Defining globalization', pp. 1480–1; and Scholte, *Globalisation: a Critical Introduction*, p. 61.
38. Thus when Scholte describes the International Criminal Court not as 'an international court' but as 'a *global suprastate* court' these implications are taken seriously: the ICC is not a court between states (though states must join the court in the first place) but an example of globality in the field of law, much as we have globality and supraterritoriality in the fields of

capitalist production, markets, environmental issues, communications, technology and so on. Scholte, *Globalisation: a Critical Introduction*, p. 73.

39. Scholte, *Globalisation: a Critical Introduction*, p. 77. G. Ó'Tuathail (1998) 'Political geography III: dealing with de-territorialization', *Progress in Human Geography* 22, no. 1.

40. I. Ali (2008) 'The Haqqani network and cross-border tension in Afghanistan', *Jamestown Terrorism Monitor* 6, no. 6; B. Fishman (2006) 'After Zarkawi: the dilemmas and future of al Qaeda in Iraq', *Washington Quarterly* 29, no. 4; M. Ranstorp (2007) 'The virtual sanctuary of al-Qaeda and terrorism in an age of globalization', in J. Eriksson and G. Giacomello (eds) *International Relations and Security in the Digital Age* (London: Routledge); and O. Roy (2004) *Globalized Islam: The Search for a New Ummah* (New York: Columbia University Press).

41. Bauman and Tester, *Conversations with Zygmunt Bauman*; Bauman, *Liquid Modernity*; Z. Bauman (2002) 'Reconnaissance wars of the planetary frontland', *Theory, Culture and Society* 19, no. 4; U. Beck (1992) *Risk Society: Towards a New Modernity* (London: Sage); U. Beck (1999) *World Risk Society* (Cambridge: Polity Press); U. Beck (2000) 'The cosmopolitan perspective: sociology of the second age of modernity', *British Journal of Sociology* 51, no. 1. M. Castells (2000) *End of Millennium (The Information Age: Economy, Society and Culture, Volume 3)*, 2nd edn (Malden, MA: Blackwell Publishing); M. Castells (2004) *The Power of Identity (The Information Age: Economy, Society and Culture, Volume 2)*, 2nd edn (Malden, MA: Blackwell Publishing); M. Castells (2000) *The Rise of the Network Society (The Information Age: Economy, Society and Culture, Volume 1)*, 2nd edn (Malden, MA: Blackwell Publishing).

42. Bauman, 'Reconnaissance wars of the planetary frontland', p. 81.

43. U. Beck (2000) 'The cosmopolitan perspective: sociology of the second age of modernity', *British Journal of Sociology* 51, no. 1; and Bauman, 'Reconnaissance wars of the planetary frontland', p. 83.

44. There is a very large literature that pertains here. For instance, M. Kaldor (1999) *New and Old Wars: Organized Violence in a Global Era* (Stanford, CA: Stanford University Press); R. Paris (2004) *At War's End: Building Peace after Civil Conflict* (Cambridge: Cambridge University Press); D. Chandler (2009) 'The global ideology: rethinking the politics of the "global turn" in IR', *International Relations* 23, no. 4; D. Chandler (ed.) (2008) *Statebuilding and Intervention: Policies, Practices and Paradigms* (London and New York: Routledge); J. Charvet and E. Kaczynska-Nay (2008) *The Liberal Project and Human Rights* (Cambridge: Cambridge University Press); D. Held (1995) *Democracy and Global Order: From the Modern State to Cosmopolitan Governance* (Cambridge: Polity Press); M. Ignatieff (2003) *Empire Lite: Nation-Building in Bosnia, Kosovo and Afghanistan* (London: Vintage); and M. Kaldor (2007) *Human Security: Reflections on Globalization and Intervention* (Cambridge: Polity Press).

45. R. Gates (2009) 'A balanced strategy: reprogramming the Pentagon for a new age', *Foreign Affairs* 88, no. 1.

46. Headquarters, United States Department of the Army and Department of the Navy, *US Counterinsurgency Manual* (Field Manual 3-24, Marine Corps Warfighting Publication 3-33.5), Dec. 2006. For the essential continuation of this policy under the Obama administration, see US Department of State, White Paper of the Interagency Group's Report on U.S. Policy toward Afghanistan and Pakistan, 29 Mar. 2009.
47. Loader and Walker, *Civilizing Security*, p. 19.
48. R.N. Haass (2008) 'The age of nonpolarity: what will follow US dominance?' *Foreign Affairs* 87, no. 3, A-M. Slaughter (2009) 'America's edge: power in the networked century', *Foreign Affairs* 88, no. 1. See also G.J. Ikenberry and A-M. Slaughter (2006) *Forging a World of Liberty Under Law: US National Security in the 21st Century* (Princeton, NJ: Woodrow Wilson School of Public and International Affairs, Princeton University).
49. Haass, 'The age of nonpolarity'; Slaughter, 'America's edge'.
50. A. Ghani and C. Lockhart (2008) *Fixing Failed States: A Framework for Rebuilding a Fractured World* (Oxford: Oxford University Press), p. 64.
51. D. Kilcullen (2006) 'Counter-insurgency *redux*', *Survival* 48, no. 4, p. 112. See also I. Duyvesteyn and M. Fumerton (2010) 'Insurgency and terrorism: is there a difference?', in C. Holmqvist-Jonsäter and C. Coker (eds) *The Character of War in the Twenty-First Century* (Abingdon: Routledge).
52. For illuminating discussion of the phenomenology of war, see S. Brighton (2011) 'Three propositions on the phenomenology of war', *International Political Sociology* 5, no. 1.
53. M. Hardt and A. Negri (2000) *Empire* (Cambridge, MA: Harvard University Press). See also D. Chandler (2008) 'The revival of Carl Schmitt in International Relations: the last refuge of critical theorists?', *Millennium: Journal of International Studies* 37, no. 1; J. Reid (2006) *The Biopolitics of the War on Terror: Life Struggles, Liberal Modernity, and the Defence of Logistical Societies* (Manchester: Manchester University Press); and W.E. Scheuerman (2006) 'Survey article: Emergency powers and the rule of law after 9/11', *Journal of Political Philosophy* 14, no. 1.
54. Hardt and Negri, *Empire*.
55. D. Chandler (2009) 'War without end: grounding the discourse of "global war"', *Security Dialogue* 40, no. 3, p. 250.
56. Hardt and Negri, *Empire*, p. 168.
57. T. Lundborg and N. Vaughn-Williams (2011) 'Resilience, critical infrastructure, and molecular security: the excess of life in biopolitics', *International Political Sociology* 5, no. 4, p. 375.
58. Ibid.
59. D. Kilcullen (2005) 'Countering global insurgency', *Journal of Strategic Studies* 28, no. 4; and Kilcullen, 'Counter-insurgency *redux*'. US Colonel John Boyd is another proponent of complexity theory as a strategic device. F. Osinga (2007) 'On Boyd, Bin Laden, and fourth generation warfare as String Theory' in J.A. Olsen (ed.) *On New Wars* (Oslo: Norwegian Institute for Defence Studies).
60. Kilcullen (2005) 'Countering global insurgency', p. 36.

61. A. Bousquet (2008) 'Chaoplexic warfare or the future of military organi-zation', *International Affairs* 84, no. 5. See also A. Bousquet (2009) *The Scientific Way of Warfare: Order and Chaos on the Battlefields of Modernity* (New York: Hurst/Colombia University Press).
62. Bousquet, 'Chaoplexic warfare or the future of military organization', p. 916.
63. D. Kilcullen (2006) *Twenty-eight Articles: Fundamentals of Company-Level Counterinsurgency* (Texas: Joint Informations Operations Center).
64. *Quadrennial Defense Review 2001*, (Washington DC: US Department of Defense, 2001).
65. Rasmussen (2007) *Risk Society at War*. See also Y.K. Heng (2006) *War as Risk Management: Strategy and Conflict in an Age of Globalised Risks, Contemporary Security Series* (Abingdon: Routledge).
66. C. Coker (2009) *War in an Age of Risk* (Cambridge: Polity Press); Heng, *War as Risk Management*; Rasmussen (2007).
67. C.J. Bickerton, P. Cunliffe and A. Gourevitch (eds) (2007) *Politics Without Sovereignty: A Critique of Contemporary International Relations* (Abingdon: University College Press).

# 4   Power in Policing Wars

1. R. Hayman (1997) *Nietzsche* (London: Phoenix), p. 1.
2. T. Hobbes (1985 [1651]) *Leviathan* (London: Penguin Classics).
3. B. Hindess (1996) *Discourses of Power: from Hobbes to Foucault* (Oxford: Blackwell), p. 137.
4. Hobbes, *Leviathan*, pp. 151–2 (chapter 10). See also C.B. Macpherson (1985) 'Introduction', in C.B. Macpherson (ed.) *Thomas Hobbes' Leviathan* (London: Penguin Classics).
5. Macpherson, 'Introduction', pp. 36–7.
6. For a brief discussion of differences in the way they use the imagery of a social contract and how they conceptualise political consent, see P. Kelly (2005) *Liberalism* (Cambridge: Polity Press), pp. 23–5.
7. Hindess, *Discourses of Power*, p. 22.
8. Ibid., p. 35. See also T. Parsons (1969) *Politics and Social Structure* (New York: Free Press).
9. Hindess, *Discourses of Power*, p. 70.
10. M. Weber (1978) *Economy and Society: An Outline of Interpretative Sociology* (Berkeley: University of California Press), p. 926. See also M. Weber (1999) *Essays in Economic Sociology*, ed. Richard Swedberg (Princeton: Princeton University Press).
11. G. Poggi (2006) *Weber: A Short Introduction* (Cambridge: Routledge), p. 90. See also H. Gerth and C. Wright Mills (eds) (1946) *From Max Weber: Essays in Sociology* (New York: Oxford University Press).
12. For an account of the role of fear in political theorising, see C. Robin (2004) *Fear: The History of a Political Idea* (New York and Oxford: Oxford University Press).
13. (Emphasis in original.) Poggi, *Weber*, p. 91.

14. Ibid., p. 95.
15. M. Mann (1986) *The Sources of Social Power, Vol. I: A History of Power from the Beginning to AD 1760* (Cambridge: Cambridge University Press), p. 10.
16. Ibid.
17. S. Toulmin (1992) *Cosmopolis: The Hidden Agenda of Modernity* (Chicago: University of Chicago Press), p. 179.
18. J. Lynn (2003) *Battle: A History of Combat and Culture* (Boulder, CO: Westview Press), p. 115.
19. A. Gat (2001) *A History of Military Thought: From the Enlightenment to the Cold War* (Oxford: Oxford University Press), pp. 382, 382–441.
20. Gat, *A History of Military Thought*, p. 382.
21. Figures taken from 'Hiroshima, Nagasaki and subsequent weapons testing' (June 2008), Official website of the World Nuclear Association, URL <http://www.world-nuclear.org/info/inf52.html>.
22. C. Coker (1998) *War and the Illiberal Conscience* (Boulder, CO: Westview Press), pp. 124–5.
23. Ibid., p. 125.
24. Ibid.
25. P. Windsor (2002) *Strategic Thinking: An Introduction and Farewell* (London: Lynne Rienner), p. 164.
26. 'Truth and Power', in M. Foucault (1980) *Power/Knowledge: Selected Interviews and Other Writings 1972–1977* (Brighton: Harvester Press), p. 121.
27. M. Foucault (1991) *Discipline and Punish: The Birth of the Prison* (Harmondsworth: Penguin), pp. 135–70, 95–231.
28. Ibid., p. 23.
29. G. Delanty (2000) *Modernity and Postmodernity: Knowledge, Power and the Self* (London: Sage), p. 1.
30. Emphasis in original. Toulmin, *Cosmopolis*, p. 185.
31. Ibid., p. 184.
32. Ibid., p. 113.
33. My emphasis. Ibid., p. 183.
34. Z. Bauman (2000) *Liquid Modernity* (Cambridge: Polity Press), pp. 11–13.
35. My emphasis. Z. Bauman (2002) 'Reconnaissance Wars of the Planetary Frontland', *Theory, Culture and Society* 19, no. 4, p. 88.
36. J.S. Nye (2004) *Soft Power: The Means to Success in World Politics* (New York: Public Affairs (Perseus Books)).
37. M. Castells (2000) *The Rise of the Network Society (The Information Age: Economy, Society and Culture, Vol. 1)*, 2nd edn (Oxford: Blackwell Publishing), p. 500.
38. Ibid., p. 446.
39. M. Castells (2000) 'Materials for an exploratory theory of the network society', *British Journal of Sociology* 51, no. 1, p. 19.
40. Ibid., p. 20.
41. A-M. Slaughter (2009) 'America's edge: Power in the networked century', *Foreign Affairs* 88, no. 1.
42. A.K. Cebrowski and J. Garstka (1998) 'Network-centric warfare: its origin and. future', *Proceedings of the US Naval Institute* 24, no. 1, pp. 28–35.

See also United States Department of Defense Report to Congress, Network Centric Warfare (Washington, DC: Department of Defense, July 2001).

43. United States (US) Department of Defense, 'The implementation of network-centric warfare', Office of Force Transformation, 7. Available at ' URL <http://www.au.af.mil/au/awc/awcgate/transformation/oft_implementation_ncw.pdf>.

44. B. Smith-Windsor (2008) *Hasten Slowly: NATO's Effects Based and Comprehensive Approach to Operations*, ed. Research Division (Rome, Italy: NATO Defense College). See also J.N. Mattis (2008) 'USJFCOM commander's guidance for effects-based operations', *Parameters* (August).

45. Speech by Arthur Cebrowski of Jan. 2003, cited in A. Bousquet (2008) 'Chaoplexic warfare or the future of military organization', *International Affairs* 84, no. 5, p. 927.

46. For an overview of use of complexity theory in politics and IR, see N. Harrison (ed.) (2006) *Complexity in World Politics: Concepts and Methods of a New Paradigm* (Albany: State University of New York Press). On complexity and strategy/war, see F. Osinga, 'On Boyd, Bin Laden, and Fourth Generation Warfare as String Theory', in J.A. Olsen (ed.) *On New Wars* (Oslo: Norwegian Institute for Defence Studies), pp. 168–97; F.P.B. Osinga (2007) *Science, Strategy and War, Strategy and History* (London and New York: Routledge). See also Bousquet, 'Chaoplexic warfare' and A. Bousquet (2009) *The Scientific Way of Warfare: Order and Chaos on the Battlefields of Modernity* (London: Hurst).

47. C. Coker (2004) *War in an Age of Risk* (Cambridge: Polity Press).

48. M. Hardt and A. Negri, (2000) *Empire* (Cambridge, MA: Harvard University Press). See also V. Jabri (2007) *War and the Transformation of Global Politics* (Basingstoke: Palgrave Macmillan); J. Reid (2007) *The Biopolitics of the War on Terror: Life Struggles, Liberal Modernity and the Defence of Logistical Societies* (Manchester: Manchester University Press).

49. Hardt and Negri, *Empire*, p. 30.

50. Ibid., pp. 135, 66.

51. Ibid, p. 40.

52. M. Foucault (2004) *Society Must Be Defended: Lectures at the Collège de France, 1975–1976*, ed. M. Bertani and trans. David Macey (London: Penguin), p. 15.

53. G. Agamben (2005) *State of Exception* (Chicago: Chicago University Press).

54. G. Agamben (1995) *Homo Sacer: Sovereign Power and Bare Life*, trans. Daniel Heller-Roazen (Stanford, CA: Stanford University Press).

55. Agamben, *State of Exception*, p. 22.

56. Examples abound: see e.g. F. Kaplan (2009) 'What are we doing in Afghanistan? We're still figuring that out', *Slate* (Washington, DC: 5 Feb. 2009), J. Klein, 'The aimless war: why are we in Afghanistan?', *Time Magazine* 11 Dec. 2008; V. Woods, 'Why are we still in Afghanistan? It's hard to tell', *The Telegraph* 14 Aug. 2009.

57. A. Heller (1999) *A Theory of Modernity* (Malden, MA: Blackwell Publishers), p. 183.

58. Bauman, 'Reconnaissance wars of the planetary frontland', p. 88.
59. UNSC Res. 1564, 8 June 2004, URL <http://www.un.org/Docs/sc/unsc_resolutions04.html>, accessed 29 Apr. 2010.
60. S. Otterman (2005) *Backgrounder: Debaathification* (Washington, DC: Council on Foreign Relations (CFR)).
61. For more detail, see T. Dodge (2005) *Iraq's Future: The Aftermath of Regime Change* (London: Routledge for IISS), pp. 9–25.
62. 'Communiqué of Afghanistan: The London Conference: Afghan Leadership, Regional Cooperation, International Partnership', London, 29 Jan. 2010. Available at URL <http://www.isaf.nato.int/images/stories/File/factsheets/Documents_Communique%20of%20London%20Conference%20on%20Afghanistan.pdf>.
63. R. Dwan and C. Holmqvist (2005) 'Major armed conflicts', in *SIPRI Yearbook 2005: Armaments, Disarmament and International Security*, ed. Stockholm International Peace Research Institute (SIPRI) (Oxford: Oxford University Press), pp. 114–16.
64. Organisation for Economic Co-operation and Development (OECD) Development Assistance Committee (DAC), Security System Reform and Governance (Paris: OECD, 2005).
65. Foucault, *Discipline and Punish*.
66. Bauman, *Liquid Modernity*, p. 11.
67. US Department of the Army Headquarters (Dec. 2006), COIN FM 3-24, p. ix.
68. IDIQ contracts are notorious for the meagre insight and control they allow the contracting party. For further discussion of the role of the global private security industry, see C. Holmqvist (2005) *Private Security Companies: The Case for Regulation* (Stockholm: Stockholm International Peace Research Institute (SIPRI)).
69. International Crisis Group (ICG), 'Reforming Afghanistan's Police', *Asia Report* (Kabul/Brussels: International Crisis Group (ICG), 30 Aug. 2007); A. Giustozzi (2009) 'The Afghan National Army: Unwarranted hope?' *RUSI Journal* 154, no. 6; R.M. Perito (2009) *Afghanistan's Police: The Weak Link in Security Sector Reform* (Washington, DC: United States Institute for Peace (USIP)).
70. Giustozzi, 'The Afghan National Army' and (ICG), 'Reforming Afghanistan's Police'.
71. N. Fekrat, 'The root causes of green on blue fire', Open Democracy website, 17 Dec. 2012. URL <http://www.opendemocracy.net/opensecurity/nasim-fekrat/root-cause-of-green-on-blue-attacks>
72. Perito, *Afghanistan's Police*.
73. R. Chandrasekaran (2004) 'Police recruits targeted in Iraq, bomb kills scores near headquarters', *Washington Post* 15 Sept.
74. Reuters, *Suicide attack kills 28 at police academy in Iraq* (Reuters, 8 Mar. 2008), available at URL <http://www.reuters.com/article/idUSTRE52151D20090308>.
75. G. Bruno (2009) 'Winning the information war in Afghanistan and Pakistan' (Washington: Council on Foreign Relations), p. 3.

76. United Nations, 'Report of the Secretary General on the situation in Afghanistan, 22 Sept. 2009', UN document number A/64/364-S/2009/475, URL <http://ods-dds-ny.un.org/doc/UNDOC/GEN/N09/515/77/PDF/N0951577.pdf?OpenElement>; ISAF, 'The International Security Assistance Force and the Afghan National Army Strength and Laydown', 22 Dec. 2009, URL <http://www.europarl.europa.eu/meetdocs/2009_2014/documents/sede/dv/sede250110natoisaffigures_/SEDE250110NATOISAFFigures_EN.pdf>. See also R. Stewart (2009) 'The irresistible illusion', *London Review of Books*, 9 July.

77. Ibid.

78. Ibid.

79. Holmqvist, *Private Security Companies*, esp. pp. 11–23. See also D. Avant (2005) *A Market for Force: The Consequences of Privatizing Security* (Cambridge: Cambridge University Press).

80. 'Military-industrial complexities', *The Economist* 29 Mar. 2003.

81. For a discussion of the problems in exerting control over an international industry, see Avant, *A Market for Force*; Holmqvist, *Private Security Companies*; and S. Chesterman and C. Lehnardt (eds) (2007) *From Mercenaries to Markets: The Rise and Regulation of Private Security Companies* (Oxford: Oxford University Press).

82. Personal communication with official at the EU Special Representative's Office, Kabul, Afghanistan, 14 Jan. 2010.

83. For more detail, see (ICG), 'Reforming Afghanistan's Police'; Bruno, 'Winning the information war'; and Perito, *Afghanistan's Police*.

84. Agence France Presse, 'We're starting "from scratch" in Afghanistan, says Holbrooke', 9 Dec. 2009, URL <http://www.afghanistannewscenter.com/news/2009/december/dec92009.html#2>, accessed 29 Apr. 2010.

85. For discussion, see Tonita Murray, 'Police-building in Afghanistan: a case study of civil security sector reform', *International Peacekeeping*, vol. 14, no. 1 (2007).

86. G. Witte (2009) 'Taliban shadow officials offer concrete alternative', *Washington Post* 8 Dec.

87. P. Cornish (2009) 'The United States and counterinsurgency', *International Affairs* 85, no. 1, p. 62; D. Ucko (2009) *The New Counterinsurgency Era: Transforming the U.S. Military for Modern Wars* (Washington, DC: Georgetown University Press).

88. United States Department of Defense, *Quadrennial Defense Review Report*, 12 Feb. 2006, URL <http://www.defense.gov/qdr/images/QDR_as_of_12Feb10_1000.pdf>.

89. Headquarters, International Security Assistance Force, Kabul, Afghanistan, 'COMISAF's Initial Assessment', 30 Aug. 2009, available at URL <http://media.washingtonpost.com/wp-srv/politics/documents/Assessment_Redacted_092109.pdf?hpid=topnews>.

90. International Security Assistance Force (ISAF), 'ISAF commander issues counterinsurgency guidance', Statement of General McChrystal 26 Aug. 2009, URL < http://www.nato.int/isaf/docu/pressreleases/2009/08/pr090827-643.html>.

91. D. Kilcullen (2006) 'Counter-insurgency *redux*', *Survival* 48, no.4, p. 123. See also Kilcullen (2005) 'Countering global insurgency', *Journal of Strategic Studies* 28, no. 4, pp. 597–697; and Kilcullen, *Twenty-eight Articles*, *Military Review* 83, no. 3, pp. 103–8.

92. Kilcullen, *Twenty-eight Articles*.

93. United Kingdom Ministry of Defence, 'Delivering Security in a Changing World', Defence White Paper, Dec. 2003, URL http://www. livreblancdefenseetsecurite.gouv.fr/IMG/pdf/whitepaper2003.pdf; T. Farrell (2008) 'The dynamics of British military transformation', *International Affairs* 84, no. 4, p. 778.

94. United Kingdom Ministry of Defence, Joint Doctrine Publication (JDP) 3-40, 'Security and Stabilisation: The Military Contribution', Nov. 2009, available at URL <http://www.mod.uk/NR/rdonlyres/C403A6C7-E72C-445E-8246-D11002D7A852/0/20091201jdp_40UDCDCIMAPPS.pdf>. United Kingdom Ministry of Defence, Joint Discussion Note 4/05, 'The Comprehensive Approach', Jan. 2006, available at URL <http://www. mod.uk/NR/rdonlyres/BEE7F0A4-C1DA-45F8-9FDC-7FBD25750EE3/0/ dcdc21_jdn4_05.pdf>.

95. Solana (2003), *A secure Europe in a better world: European Security Strategy*.

96. On the idea of security being 'cast in the language of development', see C. Coker (2009) *Rebooting the West: The US, Europe and the Future of the Western Alliance*, Whitehall Papers (Abingdon: Routledge, for Royal United Services Institute (RUSI)), p. 69. For further discussion, and diametrically opposed views of the 'security–development nexus', see R. Picciotto, F. Olonisakin and M. Clarke (2007) *Global Development and Human Security* (New Brunswick, NJ: Transaction Publishers); J. Beall, T. Goodfellow and J. Putzel (2005) 'Policy arena: Terrorism and development', *Journal of International Development* 18, no. 1, pp. 51–150; M. Duffield (2007) *Development, Security and Unending War* (Cambridge: Polity Press); and Duffield (2001) *Global Governance and the New Wars* (London: Zed Books).

97. D. Korski (2009) *Shaping Europe's Afghan Surge* (London/Brussels: European Council on Foreign Relations); G. Bruno, 'Waiting on a civilian surge in Afghanistan – Interview with John E. Herbst, Coordinator for Reconstruction and Stabilization, U.S. Department of State', 31 Mar. 2010, published on the Council of Foreign Relations (CFR), website: URL <http://www.cfr.org/publication/21785/waiting_on_a_civilian_ surge_in_afghanistan.html>.

98. Stewart, 'The irresistible illusion'.

99. D. Chandler (2008) 'Review essay: human security – the dog that didn't bark', *Security Dialogue* 39, no. 4; R. Paris (2001) 'Human security: paradigm shift or hot air?' *International Security* 26, no. 2.

100. Smith-Windsor, *Hasten Slowly*, p. 6.

101. T. Farrell and S. Gordon (2009) 'COIN machine: the British military in Afghanistan', *RUSI Journal* 154, no. 3.

102. Cornish, 'The United States and counterinsurgency', p. 75.

103. D. McKiernan (2009) 'Commander of ISAF offers a view from the ground in Afghanistan', *RUSI Journal* 27 Apr.

104. 'Iraq's liberties under threat', *The Economist* 3 Sept. 2009.
105. Swedish Television (SVT), Swedish public services national news broadcast, 'Rapport', 18 Dec. 2009.
106. For further discussion, see S. Azarbaijani-Moghaddam et al. (2008) *Afghan Hearts, Afghan Minds* (British & Irish Agencies Afghanistan Group).
107. Personal communication with official at the EU Special Representative's office, Kabul, 10 Nov. 2010.
108. Cornish, 'The United States and counterinsurgency', p. 67.

## 5 On Agency: Policing Logics and War 'Without Antagonism'

1. T. Todorov (2009) *In Defence of the Enlightenment* (London: Atlantic Books), p. 67.
2. Ibid., pp. 49–52, 64.
3. C. Coker (2009) *Rebooting the West: The US, Europe and the Future of the Western Alliance* (Abingdon: Routledge), pp. 78–9.
4. Ibid., p. 49.
5. Ibid., p. 68.
6. J. Gray (2007) *Enlightenment's Wake*, 2nd edn (Abingdon: Routledge Classics), p. 218.
7. L. Freedman (2005) 'The age of liberal wars', *Review of International Studies* 31, S1, p. 94.
8. For discussion of hypocrisy, see C. Brown (2003) 'Selective humanitarianism: in defence of inconsistency', in D. Chatterjee and D. Schein (eds) *Ethics and Foreign Intervention* (Cambridge: Cambridge University Press). See also P. Bobbitt (2007) *Terror and Consent: The Wars for the Twenty-First Century* (London: Allen Lane).
9. Todorov, *In Defence*, p. 12.
10. S. Neiman (2004) *Evil in Modern Thought: An Alternative History of Philosophy* (Princeton: Princeton University Press), p. 3.
11. C. Coker (2010) *Barbarous Philosophers* (London: Hurst), pp. 184–9.
12. Coker, *Rebooting the West*, pp. 86–7; L. Kolakowski (1989) *The Presence of Myth*, trans. Adam Czerniawski (Chicago and London: University of Chicago Press), p. 19.
13. P. Kelly (2005) *Liberalism* (Cambridge: Polity Press), p. 145.
14. Ibid., p. 154.
15. M. Walzer (1994) *Thick and Thin: Moral Argument at Home and Abroad* (Notre Dame, IN: University of Notre Dame Press); Brian Barry (1999) 'International Society from a Cosmopolitical Perspective', in D.R. Maple and T. Nardin (eds) *International Society: Diverse Ethical Perspectives* (Princeton: Princeton University Press). See also S. Lukes (2003) *Liberals and Cannibals: The Implications of Diversity* (London: Verso), pp. 36–7.
16. R. Rorty (1983) 'Postmodernist bourgeois liberalism', *Journal of Philosophy* 80, no. 10. For a critique of Rorty's hopes for a 'universal cultural condition', see Gray, *Enlightenment's Wake*, pp. 254–7.

17. C. Mouffe (2005) *On the Political* (London: Routledge), pp. 10–12.
18. T. Blair (2007) 'A battle for global values', *Foreign Affairs* Jan./Feb.
19. Prime Minister Tony Blair, Speech opening debate in the House of Commons, 18 Mar. 2003. Available at URL <http://www.guardian.co.uk/politics/2003/mar/18/foreignpolicy.iraq1>.
20. Gray, *Enlightenment's Wake*, pp. 241–3.
21. Ibid., p. 249.
22. Gray, *Enlightenment's Wake*, p. 9.
23. J.N. Shklar (1986) *Legalism: Law, Morals, and Political Trials* (Cambridge, MA: Harvard University Press), p. 1.
24. Ibid., p. vii.
25. Ibid., pp. viii–ix.
26. Ibid., p. 111.
27. Ibid., p. 21.
28. BBC Radio 4, *The Interview*, 23 Jan. 2010, available as podcast at URL <http://www.bbc.co.uk/iplayer/episode/p005vc49/The_Interview_23_01_10_Ronald_Dworkin/>. Accessed 6 May 2010.
29. Shklar, *Legalism*, p. 21.
30. See Foreword by Tracy B. Strong in Carl Schmitt ([1932] 1996) *The Concept of the Political*, trans. J.H. Tomas (Chicago: Chicago University Press).
31. H. Bielefelt (1998) 'Carl Schmitt's critique of liberalism: systematic reconstruction and countercriticism', in *Law as Politics: Carl Schmitt's Critique of Liberalism*, ed. David Dyzenhaus (Durham, NC and London: Duke University Press), pp. 24–5.
32. Schmitt, *The Concept of the Political*. See also Shklar, *Legalism*, p. 125.
33. Shklar, *Legalism*, pp. 124–27. See also E.H. Carr (2001) *The Twenty Years' Crisis, 1919–1939* (Basingstoke: Palgrave Macmillan).
34. C. Schmitt (2005) *Political Theology: Four Chapters on the Concept of Sovereignty*, trans. George Schwab (Chicago: Chicago University Press).
35. Bielefelt, 'Carl Schmitt's critique of liberalism', p. 26.
36. C. Coker (2008) *Ethics and War in the 21st Century* (Abingdon: Routledge), p. 13.
37. Ibid., p. 23.
38. See, for instance, A. Neal (2010) *Exceptionalism and the Politics of Counter-Terrorism: Liberty, Security and the War on Terror* (London: Routledge).
39. J. Huysmans (2006) 'International politics of exception: competing visions of international political order between law and politics', *Alternatives* 31; W. Scheuerman (2006) 'Survey article: emergency powers and the rule of law after 9/11', *Journal of Political Philosophy* 14, no. 1; R. van Munster (2004) 'The war on terrorism: when the exception becomes the rule', *International Journal for the Semiotics of Law* 17.
40. For an overview of such debates, see C. Brown (2006) 'Conceptions of a rule-governed international order: Europe vs. America?', *International Relations* 20, no. 3.
41. Kelly, *Liberalism*, pp. 99, 99–111.
42. Ibid., p. 102.

43. M. Hardt and A. Negri (2000) *Empire* (Cambridge, MA: Harvard University Press); M. Ignatieff (2003) *Empire Lite: Nation-building in Bosnia, Kosovo and Afghanistan* (London: Vintage).

44. J. Charvet and E. Kaczynska-Nay (2008) *The Liberal Project and Human Rights* (Cambridge: Cambridge University Press).

45. Kelly, *Liberalism*, p. 146.

46. Ibid.

47. M. Kaldor (1999) *New and Old Wars: Organized Violence in a Global Era* (Oxford: Polity Press).

48. Especially Beck (1999) *World Risk Society* (Cambridge: Polity Press).

49. D. Chandler (2009) 'The global ideology: rethinking the politics of the "global turn"' in IR', *International Relations* 23, no. 4.

50. A. Blok (2001) *Honour and Violence* (Cambridge: Polity Press).

51. G. Aijmer and J. Abbink (2000) *Meanings of Violence: A Cross-Cultural Perspective* (Oxford: Berg), p. xiii.

52. N. Rengger and C. Kennedy-Pipe (2008) 'The state of war', *International Affairs* 84, no. 5, p. 894.

53. Gray, *Enlightenment's Wake*, pp. 249–50.

54. Ibid., p. 248.

55. Ibid., p. 249.

56. (My emphasis.) J. Reid, 'The challenges of modern war', speech given at King's College London, 20 Feb. 2006.

57. For important repudiations of such views, see M. Juergensmeyer (2001) *Terror in the Mind of God: The Global Rise of Religious Violence* (Berkeley and Los Angeles: California University Press); J. Stern (2003) *Terror in the Name of God: Why Religious Militants Kill* (New York: HarperCollins).

58. J. Mueller (2004) *The Remnants of War* (Ithaca, NY: Cornell University Press).

59. Todorov, *In Defence*, p. 16.

60. O. Roy (2004) *Globalized Islam: The Search for a New Ummah* (New York: Columbia University Press).

61. Ibid. See also M. Mamdani (2005) *Good Muslim, Bad Muslim: America, the Cold War and the Roots of Terror* (New York: Three Leaves Press (Random House)); Mamdani (2005) 'Whither political Islam?' *Foreign Affairs* 84, no. 1.

62. T. Ruttig (2009) 'The other side – dimensions of the Afghan insurgency: causes, actors and approaches to "talks"' (Kabul: Afghanistan Analysts Network (ANA)).

63. United Nations Assistance Mission in Afghanistan (UNAMA), Press release, 'Special Representative of the Secretary-General met today with visiting Hezb-e-Islami delegation', 25 Mar. 2009.

64. Patten is quoted in John Gray (2008) 'Normal service will be resumed: John Gray takes issue with a politician's cheery view of the future', *The Guardian* 25 Oct. See also C. Patten (2008) *What Next? Surviving the 21st Century* (London: Allen Lane).

65. For detailed treatment of the turn of events in the months October 2002 to March 2003 and Britain's plea for a second resolution in the UN Security Council, see A. Seldon, P. Snowdon and D. Collings (2009) *Blair Unbound* (London: Simon and Schuster Ltd).

66. International Commission on Intervention and State Sovereignty (ICISS), *The Responsibility to Protect*, Report of the International Commission on Intervention and State Sovereignty, Dec. 2001. Available at URL <http://www.iciss.ca/pdf/Commission-Report.pdf>.

67. J. Crabtree (2009) 'An intellectual surge', *Prospect* no. 154, 17 Jan.

68. P. Windsor (2002) *Studies in International Relations: Essays by Philip Windsor*, ed. M. Berdal (Brighton: Sussex Academic Press), pp. 77–93.

69. C. Schmitt (2011) *Writings on War*, trans. and ed. Timothy Nunan (Cambridge: Polity Press).

70. Ibid., p. 6.

71. Ibid., p. 31.

72. Ibid., pp. 62–3.

73. Ibid., p. 65.

74. Ibid., p. 73.

75. *An Agenda for Peace: Preventive Diplomacy, Peacemaking and Peace-keeping* (Report of the Secretary-General pursuant to the statement adopted by the Summit Meeting of the Security Council on 31 Jan. 1992) (United Nations, 1992).

76. Duffield, *Development, Security and Unending War*.

77. Mouffe, *On the Political*. See also C. Mouffe (2000) *The Democratic Paradox* (London: Verso); and E. Laclau and C. Mouffe (1985) *Hegemony and Socialist Strategy: Towards a Radical Democratic Politics* (London: Verso).

78. Mouffe, *On the Political*, p. 2.

79. Mouffe, *On the Political*, p. 29.

80. Ibid., pp. 31–2.

81. B. Finel (2010) 'A substitute for victory: adopting a new counterinsurgency strategy in Afghanistan', *Foreign Affairs*, June; D. Kilcullen (2009) 'Counter-insurgency *redux*', *Survival* 48, no. 4; D. Kilcullen (2010) *Counterinsurgency* (London: Hurst); J. Nagl (2002) *Counterinsurgency Lessons from Malaya and Vietnam: Learning to Eat Soup with a Knife* (Westport, CT: Praeger); and R. Smith (2006) *The Utility of Force: The Art of War in the Modern World* (London: Penguin).

82. C. Bell (2011) 'Civilianising warfare: ways of war and peace in modern counterinsurgency', *Journal of International Relations and Development* 14.

83. United States, Department of Defense (2006) *Quadrennial Defense Review* (Washington, DC). For a theoretical exploration of the relationship between intervening forces and local populations expressed through the focus on 'strategic communication', see C. Holmqvist, 'War, 'strategic communication' and the violence of non-recognition', *Cambridge Review of International Affairs*, vol. 26, no. 4 (2013).

84. 'White Paper of the Interagency Policy Group's Report on U.S. Policy Toward Afghanistan and Pakistan', 27 Mar. 2009, URL <http://www.whitehouse.gov/assets/documents/Afghanistan-Pakistan_White_Paper.pdf>.

85. United States Joint Forces Command Joint Warfighting Center (2010) *Commander's Handbook for Strategic Communication and Communication Strategy (Version 3.0)*.

86. A. Cromartie (2012) 'Field Manual 3-24 and the heritage of counterinsurgency theory', *Millennium Journal of International Studies* 41, pp. 104–5.
87. Mouffe, *On the Political*, p. 49.
88. S. Niva (2013) 'Disappearing violence: JSOC and the Pentagon's new cartography of violence', *Security Dialogue* 40, no. 3.
89. 'Liberal societies still find the world stubbornly resistant to their own idea of war', writes Christopher Coker. Coker, *Ethics*, p. 35.

## Conclusion

1. G. Lakoff and M. Johnson (1980) *Metaphors We Live By* (Chicago: University of Chicago Press).
2. 'The Islamic Emirate of Afghanistan', Official statement 3 Nov. 2009, URL <http://www.alemarah.info/english/>.
3. P. Cornish (2009) 'The United States and counterinsurgency' *International Affairs* 85, no. 1, p. 70.
4. T. Nunan (2011) 'Translator's introduction' in C. Schmitt (ed.) *Writings on War* (Cambridge: Polity Press).
5. G. Delanty (2000) *Modernity and Postmodernity: Knowledge, Power and the Self* (London: Sage); C. Taylor (2004) *Modern Social Imaginaries* (Durham, NC: Duke University Press) and S. Toulmin (1992) *Cosmopolis: The Hidden Agenda of Modernity* (Chicago: University of Chicago Press).
6. Toulmin, *Cosmopolis*, p. 67.
7. Ibid, p. 69.
8. Z. Bauman (2002) 'Reconnaissance wars of the planetary frontland', *Theory, Culture and Society* 19, no. 4, p. 87.
9. Z. Bauman, (2000) *Liquid Modernity* (Cambridge: Polity Press), p. 11.
10. S. Toulmin (2003) *Return to Reason* (Cambridge, MA: Harvard University Press), p. 206.
11. Toulmin, *Cosmopolis*, p. 185.
12. C. Mouffe (2005) *On the Political* (New York: Routledge).

# Index

Printed by Printforce, the Netherlands